Praise
About My Fath

"Regi shows us a path that leads us
while moving them toward their own relationship with Jesus Christ.
About My Father's Business shows us the joy that comes from bringing
a kingdom purpose to our life's work."

LUIS PALAU,
PRESIDENT, LUIS PALAU EVANGELISTIC ASSOCIATION;
AUTHOR, *HIGH DEFINITION LIFE*

"I love the relevance and intelligence of Regi's message, given with
unique sensitivity. This is most certainly a refreshing and wisdom-filled
approach to an important issue. I will put this to work in my life and
recommend this book most enthusiastically!"

JIM DORNAN,
PRESIDENT, NETWORK 21, INC.;
COAUTHOR, *BECOMING A PERSON OF INFLUENCE* WITH JOHN MAXWELL

"There may be no greater opportunity to reach our culture for Christ
than through the marketplace. Regi has been there, done that, and he
shares his wealth of wisdom and experience. I have the privilege of rec-
ommending this book wholeheartedly."

RON BLUE,
PRESIDENT, CHRISTIAN FINANCIAL PROFESSIONALS NETWORK

"Regi Campbell's process for identifying and nurturing workplace relationships will help every believer more intentionally and effectively
impact their spheres of influence. Well done, Regi!"

OS HILLMAN,
PRESIDENT, INTERNATIONAL COALITION OF WORKPLACE MINISTRIES
AND MARKETPLACE LEADERS

"Regi Campbell hits the bull's-eye. *About My Father's Business* is a practical book that needs to be in the hands of every serious Christian
longing to make a difference in their work life."

CHIP INGRAM,
CEO AND PRESIDENT, WALK THRU THE BIBLE;
TEACHING PASTOR, LIVING ON THE EDGE RADIO

"Regi Campbell has done us a great favor by writing this book. *About
My Father's Business* is for every Christian who wants to obey Christ
and take His commands seriously. Read it and use it. You will be
blessed."

MICHAEL YOUSSEF, PHD,
AUTHOR, *DIVINE DISCONTENT*

"Regi has captured God's heart for every Christian businessman to be a light in the marketplace. The process is simple and effective. This book will make a real impact for the kingdom of God."

BRUCE R. WITT,
DIRECTOR OF FIELD MINISTRY,
CONNECTING BUSINESS MEN TO CHRIST

"As a friend and business associate, I have admired Regi Campbell's committed and maturing faith for nearly three decades. In *About My Father's Business*, Regi's approach is open and nonjudgmental, and his writing is inspirational. I highly recommend this book to any Christian seeking more out of his or her workday than a paycheck or a promotion."

GARY M. PARSONS,
CHAIRMAN, XM SATELLITE RADIO

"For many years workplace and ministry have been viewed as entirely separate, almost like the church and state. Now, as men and women begin to see their workplace as their greatest field for harvest, we're entering a revival. Regi's work is a valuable tool for any Christian ready to touch their marketplace for God."

PAT GELSINGER,
AUTHOR, BALANCING YOUR FAMILY, FAITH AND WORK;
SR. VP AND CTO, INTEL CORPORATION

"Regi helps you get 'the monkey on your back'—a sense of 'ought to' about sharing your faith in the marketplace. His approach is practical and wise, one he has modeled for years. He's one of the finest mentors to young businessmen I've known, and this book will multiply what he has already done in the lives of individuals he has mentored."

G. BRYANT WRIGHT,
SENIOR PASTOR, JOHNSON FERRY BAPTIST CHURCH

"For the last ten years I've watched Regi in the boardroom, leading a company or investing in start-ups, impacting those around him for Christ. Now he's written the book that reveals practical, easy to follow steps so we can do it, too."

CHARLIE PAPARELLI,
VENTURE CAPITALIST AND PRESIDENT, HIGH TECH MINISTRIES

"*About My Father's Business* is a practical strategy for being intentional with our lives between Sundays. Regi is the CEO with the vision and experience to wisely get us on the right track."

DARYL HEALD,
PRESIDENT, GENEROUS GIVING

Endorsements continued on page 239

ABOUT MY
FATHER'S
BUSINESS

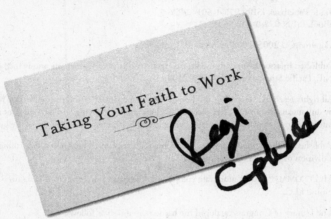

Taking Your Faith to Work

REGI
CAMPBELL

Foreword by ANDY STANLEY

MULTNOMAH
BOOKS

ABOUT MY FATHER'S BUSINESS

All Scripture quotations, unless otherwise indicated, are taken from the Holy Bible, New International Version®. NIV®. Copyright © 1973, 1978, 1984 by International Bible Society. Used by permission of Zondervan Publishing House. All rights reserved. Scripture quotations marked (NKJV) are taken from the New King James Version®. Copyright © 1982 by Thomas Nelson Inc. Used by permission. All rights reserved.

Details in some anecdotes and stories have been changed to protect the identities of the persons involved.

Trade Paperback ISBN 978-1-60142-226-2
eBook ISBN 978-0-307-56358-3

Copyright © 2005, 2009 by James R. Campbell

Published in association with the literary agency of Sanford Communications Inc., 6406 N.E. Pacific Street, Portland, OR 97213.

Published in the United States by Multnomah, an imprint of the Crown Publishing Group, a division of Penguin Random House LLC, New York.

MULTNOMAH® and its mountain colophon are registered trademarks of Penguin Random House LLC.

The Library of Congress cataloged the hardcover edition as follows:
Campbell, Regi.
    About my Father's business / Regi Campbell.
      p. cm.
    Includes bibliographical references.
    ISBN 1-59052-407-1
    1. Employees—Religious life. 2. Witness bearing (Christianity) 3. Work—Religion aspects—Christianity. 4. Christian Life. I. Title.
    BV4593.C26 2005
    248.8'8—dc22

                                                                    2004021726

Printed in the United States of America
2017

10 9 8 7

SPECIAL SALES
Most Multnomah books are available at special quantity discounts when purchased in bulk by corporations, organizations, and special-interest groups. Custom imprinting or excerpting can also be done to fit special needs. For information, please e-mail specialmarketscms@penguinrandomhouse.com or call 1-800-603-7051.

This book is dedicated to my friend and brother Craig Callaway.
It was through his spiritual journey from apathy to excelling
Christian that most of the principles in this book were validated.
And it is because of his encouragement that there are words
on this paper and this book is in your hands.
A man will never have a better friend
than the one he helps find the Answer to life.
And I will never have a better friend than Craig.

CONTENTS

FOREWORD

DOING WHAT I DO, I MEET SHARP BUSINESS PEOPLE FROM ALL over the world. And from my involvement with top ministry leaders, I meet people who have a passion to share Christ. In Regi Campbell, you get both.

When my pastor first suggested that Margaret and I start a small group and Regi Campbell and his wife became a part of it, I immediately saw that Regi had both business wisdom and spiritual passion. I knew that he was involved in the lay leadership of our church and that our pastor, Andy Stanley, often sought Regi's insight on big decisions. But as I got to know Regi personally, I began to understand why. He thinks clearly; he speaks clearly; he speaks from experience; and there's a ton of wisdom in what he has to say.

But the side of Regi that is even more impressive is his heart for the people that he works with. Here's an "entrepreneur of the year"…a leader with a lot of success in the business world, asking the people in our group to pray for people on "his list." I now recognize that list as his "intentionality map" (he will give you the details as you read *About My Father's Business*). He would ask us to pray for people that he had developed relationships with…to pray that God would move them "the next step" toward excelling in Christ. As the months went on, I gained a very healthy respect for Regi's insights and wisdom. Some of the people at my company, the Injoy Group, had also come to know Regi, and we ultimately invited him to help us shape Injoy's strategy and plans to help churches and business people to be more effective in the marketplace for Christ. Regi gave us his time because he so badly wants to see business people wake up to the opportunity that they have to influence people for Christ right where they are, every day at work.

If you're a business person and you've been looking for someone to show you what to do next in "taking your faith to work," this book is for you. If your husband or wife is a business person, this book will challenge them to "get in the game," but in a way that is smart and effective. And if you are a pastor, this book can provide the business people in your church with a "track to run on" for effective evangelism and discipleship in the marketplace.

John C. Maxwell
Author and Founder, The INJOY Group

FOREWORD

FOR THE PAST NINE YEARS I HAVE LEANED HEAVILY ON THE
wisdom and advice of Regi Campbell. Often I catch myself asking, *What would Regi do in this situation?* And I'm not alone. Over
the years Regi Campbell has poured his life and wisdom into
dozens of professional men and women. The time he invests in
others flows from his conviction that his own success in business is something to be stewarded rather than hoarded.

When Regi mentioned that he was interested in writing a
book, I connected him with my publisher, Don Jacobson, president of Multnomah. When Don finished talking with Regi, he
called me. "Wow!" Don said. "Not only do I want to publish his
book, I want to sit down and pick his brain about the publishing business."

I wasn't surprised. Regi's business intuition, along with his
uncanny ability to read people, positions him as a coveted mentor for anyone who is attempting to take his or her company to
the next level.

But there is more to Regi than insight and business acumen. Like a growing number of professionals in this country, Regi sees the marketplace as a platform for ministry. Thus the title of his book.

Regi has been about his Father's business for more than twenty years in a variety of corporate environments. He has waded through personal issues of reputation and perception. He has confronted the barriers posed by policy and procedure. And he is well aware of the legal ramifications of bringing one's faith to work. When it comes to ministering in the marketplace, Regi is a decorated veteran. And like every veteran, he has a story to tell—a story that offers value and insight to every professional who has a passion to leverage his career for kingdom purposes.

I know there are a dozen or more books on this topic; it's something of a publishing trend. But the content of this book is anything but trendy. This is meat and potatoes for any man or woman who is serious about being an ambassador for Christ at work. For as you are about to discover, Regi successfully dismantles the artificial wall we have erected for ourselves between work and ministry.

In *About My Father's Business*, Regi Campbell provides you with a strategy for assessing your workplace, identifying your opportunities, neutralizing primary obstacles, and boldly enjoying the mission God has called you to. I believe the message of this book has the potential to fuel-inject the marketplace ministry movement—a movement to which God has called every one of us who gets up and goes to work.

Andy Stanley

THE MONKEY

NO DOUBT YOU KNOW THE MONKEY...PERHAPS ALL TOO WELL. Every sincere Christian is familiar with him. He's most noticeable on Mondays, especially if the sermon that Sunday was about being a vibrant witness for Jesus Christ.

The monkey shows up just as you're getting settled in for a new week. As you finish up your morning coffee, you're pretty pumped about being one of the good guys—a Christian—at work. Then one of your coworkers stops by to share a new joke and to fill you in on the wild party he had that weekend. As every illicit detail is described, you think of the sermon you heard the day before. Suddenly, you feel the monkey—the unmistakable weight of responsibility to stand up for your faith in a world that needs God.

If you're like me, you'll start to rationalize with the monkey. *Surely, I'm not just supposed to start talking about God now…right in the middle of a story like this!* Gradually, the unspoken dialogue evolves into a theological discussion. *Does this person really think*

*I'm just another one of the guys? If so, then I must not be much of a
witness. Maybe I'm not as spiritual as I thought. Maybe my salvation
didn't really stick.* Since you obviously haven't been a very good
witness up until now, you can't help feeling some pressure to
give the right response—one that would honor God and let this
guy know whose side you're on. Unsure of what to do, however,
you fake your best laugh at the joke, despite its crude overtones.
After all, you don't want to alienate yourself from someone who
obviously needs God. Even Jesus wouldn't do that.

Later that day you're sitting in a strategy session to brain-
storm ways the company can reduce turnover among its
employees. You can't help recalling the Christian book you finished recently about how to treat people the way that Jesus did.
You remember how moved you were when you read about God
intervening to help the people who put Him first. You would
love to be part of something like that. Maybe God showed you
those principles so you could suggest them in this meeting.
Maybe it would start a new movement in your workplace.
Maybe that's part of God's purpose for your life's work.

Then again, maybe they'll just think you're crazy. They
might laugh behind your back for months. You might lose all
respect at work, and along with it any chance for having any
Christian influence. Besides, maybe it's God's purpose that you
just earn a good living for your family without rocking the boat.
The monkey feels even heavier for the moment.

The monkey can show up just about anywhere. It's the burden we Christians feel when we remember we're supposed to be
making disciples. But all along we're struggling to understand
what it means to share our faith in a country where it's politically
incorrect to "impose" our beliefs on others. So we learn to work
within the boundaries. It's okay to mention God, just don't talk

about Jesus. It's okay to do Christmas as long as it's about Santa and winter rather than what's central to our faith.

As Christians, we get pretty good at blending in. And for a while, the monkey goes away.

As Christians, we get pretty good at blending in.

Then along comes a speaker at church telling stories about boldly sharing his faith on an airplane or something. We hear of people instantly turning to Christ, all because of the faith of someone who was willing to risk it all for God. We can't help wondering if we're supposed to be doing something like that…something profound—something God-sized—with our lives. Maybe being a Christian in the workplace should look a little more like that guy on the airplane. After all, he had only a couple of hours to operate; we've got forty every week. You have to wonder if we're really doing all we're supposed to as Christians. Is God truly pleased with our lives?

Wait a minute. There I go again, overthinking things. Enough already. Spirituality is important, but it's not everything. All things in moderation. Besides, God just wants me to be at peace.

Then again, maybe sharing my faith in my workplace *is* what it's all about. After all, here I am, a pretty serious Christian, and I'm surrounded by people who don't really know the difference between religion and a relationship with the living Christ. I'm supposed to be a light in the darkness. I've been charged with carrying out the great commission. There's got to be something I should be doing around my coworkers. Surely He didn't intend for me just to blend in.

The monkey can make you feel *overwhelmed*—there's a burden of responsibility when you're talking about someone's eternal destination. The monkey can make you feel *guilty*—what if you are denying your faith by not speaking more openly about it in the workplace? The monkey can make you feel *frustrated*—it's hard to know how to share your faith without looking like a superstitious simpleton to all your coworkers. What good would it do for God or your career if you lose your credibility?

When I first started to experience all this confusion years ago, my first instinct was to pretend the monkey wasn't there. After all, I looked pretty good compared to most of the other Christians I knew. But the more serious I became about my faith, the harder the challenge was to ignore. When you drive from a men's prayer breakfast to an office that's hostile toward God, the contrast is undeniable. It's hard to gloss over the fact that you possess a treasure that could change the lives of everyone around you, if only you were willing to share it.

I've even tried running away from the monkey. What better way to exercise my faith than to start my own "Christian" company? And if I surrounded myself with enough Christians, maybe the tension of having to deal with all those non-Christians would go away. But it didn't. Deep inside, I still knew there were people out there who needed to hear about the God who runs deeper than religion.

So, over the years, I've emerged from that struggle over how to share my faith in the workplace with a clear picture of what it means to be about my Father's business. I have learned that there is no greater calling than to make my workplace my mission field.

> There is no greater calling than to make
> my workplace my mission field.

In the pages that follow, I've distilled what I've learned into a strategic method for sharing Jesus Christ in your workplace. You are about to discover some eye-opening principles that will change your whole approach to your work and to your faith— no more uncertainty about when it's appropriate to speak up or whether your timing is right. I will also share a powerful assessment model that can help you identify the most strategic opportunities in your workplace. You will be able to see more clearly where God is calling you to focus your efforts—no more awkwardness or blurting out holy hand grenades in a desperate attempt to bring God into the picture.

Best of all, I want to share some of the true stories of God at work where I work. You see, this is not evangelism theory or theology. This is a very practical account from someone who's been there. I went from being a fellow struggler to a confident follower of Christ who has learned when it's time to speak up...and what to do in the meantime. I've seen the most unlikely agnostics move into a vibrant relationship with Christ. This is not because I'm a great evangelist, but because God came alongside me to show me what to do. I had made "sharing my faith" into a gut-wrenching event. But now I've learned that I am most effective when I follow a slow, natural, even comfortable process. I feel like a load of guilt has been taken off my back and that being an influence for Christ in the marketplace is now something that's doable!

And now I want to show you how you can do it, too. Because you, too, can be a confident, effective witness for Jesus Christ where you work. And when you are, you will have the joy of going to work each day knowing that you are truly about your Father's business.

THE CURSE?

WORK.

It seems destined to be a four-letter word. No matter how you spell it—job, career, calling—it still has *curse* written all over it. Maybe that's just the way it's supposed to be. After all, it was the original curse word, as Adam first lived out the consequences of his cursed life by working the land for food. To this day, work ranks among the leading obstacles in many people's lives.

It seems the dreams of most working people revolve around arriving at a place where they'll no longer have to go to work. That's not to say we don't enjoy some of the challenges along the way. But if you could dig beneath the surface, the primary objective of most people's career is to eliminate the need for it.

The primary objective of most people's career
is to eliminate the need for it.

Advertisers play to this sentiment, tantalizing their target audiences with depictions of financial freedom and absolute autonomy. Statewide lotteries are funded, one dollar at a time, by the pipe dreams of would-be early retirees. While money is the number one obsession in our culture, the ultimate end of wealth is emancipation from the workplace.

It is common sentiment that work is something to be avoided.

Work is universally portrayed as something that gets in the way of all the other things we'd rather be doing. Work calls the shots. It's the factory whistle that awakens us each day from the dream of a life of leisure. Work drags us from our homes and subjects us to traffic jams and the shark-infested waters of competition. Work drops us back home in a heap at the end of the day, or at the end of a long business trip. Work tells us where we can live, what we should wear, when we can go on vacation, and how much we can spend in between. Wherever our hearts turn in life, work is there dictating the pace and saying yes or no to our heartfelt passions and desires.

WE ARE WHAT WE DO?

As young children, we are encouraged to dream of what we want to be when we grow up. Our educational system is oriented around shaping us into one of the molds that will define us as bachelors in business administration, economics, English, science, or education. Eventually, we refine our identity to the point that we fit nicely into one of the categories that can be found in the yellow pages, or a title on the organizational chart of the company where we work. And after all is settled, one of the first questions people ask when they meet us is, "What do you do?"

In our culture, we are defined by what we do. And everything else revolves around it. Wherever the career opportunities take us is where we raise our families, attend our churches, and join the neighborhood pool. What we do precedes who we are.

There's just one problem. We don't want anything to tell us what to do. We love autonomy. So, in allegiance to our human nature, we make it our goal to cheat the system. We work for rapid promotions, we invest for early retirement, and we play the lottery to increase our chances of getting our freedom as soon as we can...winning back control of our lives while we are still young enough to enjoy it.

As the headline for a retirement fund ad put it, "Life is two periods of play separated by forty years of work."

So work is a curse to be endured. At least, that's how the average person views work.

BUT WHAT ABOUT CHRISTIANS?

Surely, we Christians hold a more enlightened view of work. We have beheld the truth that work was ordained by God even before Adam and Eve invented apple pie. We know that God Himself worked and called it good. We embrace the ideal of working "heartily, as to the Lord" (Colossians 3:23, NKJV). We read the Bible and learn that God uses work to mold our character and meet our needs. We understand that work will be one of our joyous assignments in Heaven, not just the lot of those condemned to the other place.

We have learned that work is not really a bad thing in God's eyes.

And yet, when it comes to being a Christian at work, many believers don't feel that way at all. We understand that work is not quite the curse we once thought it was. But in our quest to be a beacon of light to a lost world, we often see work as something that gets in the way. We long to live out our faith Monday through Saturday, but we have to go to work instead. We dream of how effective we could be for the Lord...if it weren't for this lousy job.

> We long to live out our faith Monday through Saturday, but we have to go to work instead.

Somehow, we develop an either/or mentality: I can either be in the secular work world or I can be in ministry, but not in both. We have bifurcated work into these two distinct realms rather than seeing the both/and possibility. What if we could be in the marketplace *and* be in ministry at the same time? Suppose we saw our workplace as our church and our jobs as our ministry. Suppose we went after our workplace ministry with the same fervor and passion as a twenty-six-year-old youth pastor just out of seminary.

The idea of being in ministry at work was something I had shied away from. I had been a pretty good church member, but work was a whole different ball game. Let me tell you my story, and you'll see why ministry was pretty far from my thinking in my early career.

I was a rising star at AT&T. At age thirty, I was promoted to division level, one of the youngest ever. At thirty-three, I was to be nominated for the company's Sloan Fellowship Program, a key prerequisite for moving up the corporate ladder.

But on the heels of a transfer from Charlotte, North Carolina, to Atlanta, I experienced a major disruption. What had been a smooth career path suddenly became rocky. At the same time, my marriage was in trouble, the consequence of eleven years of putting my career above everything else. Realizing that I couldn't hold my life together by myself any longer, I turned to God for help. On a starry night I will never forget, I walked out in the backyard and told God I was finally His. I gave it all up to Him. "It's You and me, Lord," I said. "I am going public with my faith. I'm going to stand for something. Whatever happens, happens!"

I was changed forever that night. God gave me a new heart and a new attitude based on a deep gratitude for His forgiveness and His acceptance. I knew that I was loved for the first time in my life. I was ready to live for Him 24-7, but from that point forward, it got even harder to live a dual life.

Away from the office, I devoured Christian books and Bible teaching to feed my spiritual growth. At work, however, I struggled to live out my faith in a world that seemed completely disconnected from the God I was getting to know. I don't mean I was struggling with sin and backsliding. For once, that wasn't the problem. It's just that I lived in a spiritual place that had meaning and purpose, yet I worked in an earthly place that now seemed antiquated and irrelevant. I wanted to move on to my new life, but this old environment—work—kept getting in the way.

As much as I tried, I couldn't seem to reconcile those two worlds. Attempts to tell my story and share my faith at work were awkward. And my efforts to operate by biblical principles seemed hypocritical in light of the old reputation that still followed me around. I wanted people to see a reflection of God in me, but I was convinced all they could see was the same old me on a new religious kick. I felt shackled to my past.

I was so grateful for God's forgiveness, I could hardly contain myself. He had started to restore my marriage; I was in love with my wife and kids in a way that I hadn't known before. And I was in love with God. I needed to do something bold. I kept dreaming of how effectively I could serve Him, if I could just get away from my job.

Inevitably, I concluded that I should leave the old world and relocate permanently to a different one. After all, the disciples left their nets to follow Jesus.

So I left the world of AT&T behind and started a consulting business where I could live out my new life-purpose statement: "to glorify God by teaching biblical principles to sales and marketing executives."

At last I was free to be the new me without the constant reminders of what I once was. I could freely talk about my faith without apprehension that I might look like a hypocrite on religious dope. I was free to play on my Christian playground without fear of interruption.

At least, that's how I saw it.

But as I look back on that experience, I've come to realize I may have walked out on an incredible opportunity. What better place to fulfill my new life-purpose statement than as Division Manager of Sales at AT&T Information Systems? We had thousands of employees, hundreds of offices...there was unlimited potential. The more I understand about how God uses Christians in the marketplace, the more I realize that I had been sitting on a spiritual gold mine back at AT&T. I just didn't recognize it.

> I had been sitting on a spiritual gold mine back at AT&T.
> I just didn't recognize it.

TWO LIVES BECOME ONE

Over the past two decades, I've had successes both in business and in helping business people come to faith. Ironically, it took only one year for God to use the consulting business I started to lead me right back to a leadership role in the marketplace—the world of profit and loss, hiring and firing, performance reviews and sales incentives. God was faithful to bring me back to these work environments because that's where effective ministry can occur. And after being in several situations that more closely resembled the one I left, I eventually figured out how to reconcile those two worlds into one.

Surprisingly, God didn't need me to be a perfect Christian with a long history of faultless integrity. He just wanted me to seek His kingdom and His righteousness while I excelled at my work, family, church, and community life. Sometimes it's enough if we're willing just to stick around and let people watch God take over our hearts. That simple example, with all its awkwardness and blemishes, can be the most convincing evidence of God they will ever see.

I've now spent more than twenty years helping people see how relevant God is to our everyday lives. As a friend of mine says, we need to "turn Bible leather into shoe leather"…to get God out of the stained glass and into our relationships.

After all those experiences, I'm left with a haunting question. How many Christians are ignoring the monkey? How many would like to make a difference, but just don't know what to do? How many are surrounded by a ripe harvest, but just don't know how to recognize it?

I mentor eight young men each year, so I'm continually around young Christians who remind me of myself twenty years ago. They struggle with living out their faith at work. I'll bet I've had a dozen guys ask me about quitting work and going to seminary or starting their own "Christian" business. And others simply settle for the compromise of living a dual life, confining the focus and energy of their Christianity to church activities while keeping a low spiritual profile at work.

They're not alone. As I look across the landscape of believers today, I see a lot of Christians wrestling with what a true disciple of Christ should look like in the workplace. Somewhere along the way, we've lost our vision for how Christ would conduct ministry at work. Over the last century, the business culture has been constantly reinventing itself with new technologies and innovations. But Christianity, it seems, has been left behind. That's not to say there aren't Christians in the marketplace. It's just that they lack the zeal and confidence that's truly representative of what God is doing inside them. Or they just don't know what God would have them do.

We've lost our vision for how Christ would conduct ministry at work.

The problem is that when a person begins to grow in his passion for God, it creates tension at work. We know how to express our true feelings in church or in private, but how should we act around the office or in the field or in the factory? What does it look like? Should we come on strong and risk offending people? Or should we take the long road and hope our faith just rubs off on others over time?

It only takes one or two awkward experiences for Christians to realize that an enthusiasm for God doesn't exactly blend seamlessly into the American business culture. We learn quickly that you can't be careless about it. Subconsciously, it's easier to suppress our kingdom calling in order to ease the clash of cultures we face each day. When we're not sure what to do, it's safer to do nothing. Why rock the boat?

Eventually, Christians tend to adopt one of two solutions to relieve the tension they feel at work. They either run or they hide.

The *run* response comes from the idea that it would just be easier to make a clean break—to start over in a new environment or to withdraw completely by enrolling in seminary and going into ministry full-time. There was an element of this driving my decision to leave AT&T and start a consulting business. Rather than make my current workplace my ministry, I ran away to create an environment that was more comfortable and controllable.

The *hide* response is nothing less than a subtle surrender of the mission. Unsure of how to interface our exuberance for God with a workplace that may not appreciate it, we tone it down around the office. And the fervor we feel on Sunday gets squelched a little from Monday to Friday. Essentially, we hide our true self from the work world.

Somehow we can't quite grasp the vision of our work as an opportunity to share our faith. I'm the first to admit that it doesn't come easily. But after twenty years of practicing market-place ministry and teaching these principles to others, I've come up with an approach that will give you a clear vision for your calling to be about our Father's business at work.

You see, regardless of how uncomfortable the tension may seem now, God doesn't call us to run. And He doesn't teach us to hide. Chances are He wants to use you right where you are. How else will people who don't go to church find out about the relationship their Heavenly Father longs to have with them? It's not like it's talked about in the places they frequent. But because of your unique position in their lives, you have the opportunity to be someone God can use to tell them. And it doesn't have to feel awkward. When you understand your role in the process, it can be one of the most natural and rewarding experiences you will ever know.

The disciples may have dropped their nets, but they didn't run *or* hide. They spent the next several years living and ministering among many of the same people that already knew them. Often, we must prove faithful in our current mission field before God will entrust a new one to us. And as we'll see, sometimes God does powerful things when we simply hang around long enough to allow others a chance to witness the transformation in our lives.

In the pages that follow, I'd like to give you a step-by-step plan for how you can begin the work of ministry right where you are. You will learn a strategy for assessing your workplace, identifying your opportunities, neutralizing the primary obstacles, and boldly enjoying the mission God gives you.

Work is not a curse for Christians. It's a place where you live out your faith, reflecting what God is doing in your life. In light of eternity, the ministry you accomplish at work can be more important than the money you earn or the career you sustain. And once you see the impact God can have through you on the job, you will never look at your workplace the same again.

> Work is a place where you live out your faith, reflecting what God is doing in your life.

If you want to experience true joy in your life (both this one and the next), if you want to do work that really matters, if you want to have peace in your life all the time, and if you want to have a fulfilling work life, commit yourself to the process that I'm going to show you.

Go to your job and do great work, but while you're at it, be about our Father's business.

You can do this!

AT WORK...
ON TWO JOBS!

SO HOW DO YOU RESOLVE THE TENSION BETWEEN THE PERSON you are spiritually and the person you are at work? How can you be just as passionate about your relationship with God on Wednesday afternoon as you are on Sunday morning? How can you live out in the workplace what you really believe in your heart without making a complete idiot of yourself and destroying your reputation?

How does one come to be less worried about what other people think and more interested in what our heavenly Father thinks?

How does one come to be less worried about what other people think and more interested in what our heavenly Father thinks?

That's the question I began wrestling more than two decades ago. Since that time, I've discovered not only that it can be done, but it's what God intends for us as Christians. In fact, I've seen God make my career and business endeavors flourish, while at the same time allowing me to introduce the most unlikely souls to Christ.

Earlier, I told you about leaving AT&T and starting a consulting business. That business flourished, and after just a few months, I was learning that God has a lot more to do with the success of a business than I ever dreamed. My first client literally walked in the door while I was making sales calls like there was no tomorrow and getting consistently rejected.

My second client insisted on a six-month retainer, which I thought was cool but weird. Their offer almost matched our monthly living expenses. Go God!

Then I made a proposal to help a small technology start-up. The proposal evolved into a dialogue about me coming on board with the company. I sought the counsel from some of my closest friends, who gave me some tough but godly advice. "You were successful at AT&T, but you did it the world's way. Now you've got a new heart; go out there and do it His way. You've been teaching Christian principles in the sales and marketing workplace. Now go demonstrate them."

So I agreed to head up this three-person start-up company. We developed a corporate value system—a set of commitments that outlined how we would treat each other, our employees, our customers, our vendors, and our shareholders. And we attempted to really live it out. The goal was for each of us to live our faith every day at work, and to create an environment of love, service, acceptance, and caring. It wasn't a Christian company

(I'm not sure there is such a thing), but it was certainly a Christian-friendly place, where people were respected, loved, and challenged. The company blossomed, sometimes in spite of my decision making. Six years later, it was sold to a large public company in the telecommunications industry for a lot of money.

A couple of years later, the team that built that company rallied around a new idea and started another company, using the same value system and attempting to create the same kind of environment for employees and customers. Four years later, that company was sold for a lot of money. People began calling me an entrepreneur, although I've never felt that I deserved that label. But I have tried to be a marketplace minister. I have been intentional about making a difference for Christ in the workplace in every business that I've been involved in.

You see, my kingdom purpose became my first priority. I want to love and serve people and influence them to move one step closer to Christ as I go about my job. Before, I went about my job and tried to use people to help me get what I wanted at work. Christ didn't enter into the picture unless there was a problem. Do you see the difference?

I once heard a speaker say that a secular endeavor, approached from a spiritual perspective, is spiritual; while a spiritual endeavor, approached from a secular perspective, is secular. If I approach my job motivated to love and serve people for the purpose of influencing them for Christ, then I've been more spiritual in my motive than a senior pastor who forgets about the people and approaches running his church like running a business. "How are the numbers?" "How many did we have in Sunday school?" "What do we have to do to get that capital campaign in gear?"

It's all about the "why"—the motive in our hearts. When we truly embrace the notion that God is first in our lives, and we decide to approach our jobs with God-motives at the top of our lists, our whole perspective on work changes.

And what's been amazing to me is how my work performance seems to improve and the business results get better at the same time! Jesus explained this when He said "Seek *first* his kingdom and his righteousness, and all these things will be given to you as well" (Matthew 6:33, italics added).

To God, work is a superimportant environment because we are in close, constant contact with tons of people. In fact, it's the environment where we have the *most* contact with the *most* people, simply because we spend more of our time there than we spend anywhere else. Remember, people matter more to God than anything else. How do we know that? Because people are made in God's own image. God sacrificed His only Son and watched Him die...for what? For people. His kingdom is about people. Period.

His kingdom is about people. Period.

You see, if you're a Christian, then you're on a mission from God. Whether you embrace it or not, God has taken possession of your life in order to advance His kingdom by helping people find Him one step at a time. The more you understand about His agenda for your career, the better you will be able to work alongside Him to fulfill it.

COMPARTMENTALIZING OUR CHRISTIANITY

Why is it so difficult to reconcile these two worlds—our spiritual life and our work life? Why is it our instinct to run or to hide?

In essence, it's because we live our lives in compartments. Like sections of the newspaper, our lives divide neatly into categories. There's the business side of life, the people section, sports, travel, and religion. They don't overlap, and they don't interfere with each other.

A little over a century ago, things were very different. Up until the late 1800s, we were primarily a collection of agricultural communities. Life revolved around the ebb and flow of cultivating and harvesting. People back then lived like an agricultural community. And they thought like an agricultural community. There were exceptions, but for the most part, the mind-set was agricultural.

Just try to grasp how much that differs from the way we think today. When you live in an agricultural world, you have a completely different view of control. When you farm or hunt for a living, you are not in control of your progress. Essentially, you live a reactive life. When winter begins to thaw, you plow and plant. When the rain dries up, you irrigate. When the days are longer, you work longer. When the fruit begins to ripen, you harvest. And when calamity strikes, you pray. As a farmer friend told me several years ago, "The land and the weather determine what I do each day."

Then along came the industrial revolution. Almost overnight, the expectations on the workforce changed. What was once determined by chance was now rigorously controlled by the speed of the assembly line conveyors. Suddenly, progress was fused to performance. The day's tasks were no longer passively determined by the land or the weather, but carefully planned by systems designers. Rain or shine, progress marched on. Even the length of a day was now determined by the shift scheduler.

In time, the benchmark for vocational activity was defined as the window between 9 a.m. and 5 p.m., Monday through Friday—forty hours around which the rest of life revolved.

With that shift to industrialization, our culture became more compartmentalized. We became schedule oriented. Everything we do must take its place on the calendar without violating the forty-hour window. Whether it's being a homeowner with a yard to maintain or a consumer with bills to pay, you must find a compartment in which to be that person. Our lives became defined by the various tasks we perform. And the clock became the taskmaster.

Even the activities that reflect our inner identity must assume time slots on the calendar. If you are a spouse or a parent, there are special compartments of time for being that. If playing golf or going to the theater are expressions of your personality, you must either schedule those events or you won't do them....tacitly giving up a part of your identity. Whatever you are must be given a compartment on the calendar.

The natural tendency is that we can become defined more by what we do than by who we are. Christianity becomes not so much about what we believe, but about what we *do* on Sunday morning.

We can become defined more by what we do than by who we are.

There's just one problem with this mind-set. The attributes of your inner person don't fit into compartments. Your personality type and the roles you play follow you wherever you go. If you are a born leader, you will always interpret the world through those eyes. If you assume the role of mother, it will color every other experience you have. Outgoing or shy, Republican or Democrat, liberal or conservative, naturalist or urbanite, the factors that define our identity don't fit into time slots. They bleed over into everything we do.

True Christianity doesn't fit into a compartment either. Because being a Christian is a personal attribute, an identity, like male or female. It's also a worldview. It touches everything you do. It shows up in every interaction you have, no matter where you go. Once we belong to God, we can't leave that identity or that relationship in our closet, like the shirt we chose not to wear today. He's there all the time—with us, in us, wanting to live through us.

Therein lies the tension between work and faith. The industrialized work world requests a sanitized environment where productivity can be maximized. Relationships are to be professional and distraction free. Progress cannot be compromised by the agenda of one's personal beliefs. Say what you want at home or at church. Just don't wear it on your sleeve on Monday morning.

But Christianity has the opposite intention. "You are the light of the world. A city on a hill cannot be hidden," Jesus said (Matthew 5:14). By nature, it declares exemption from compartmentalization. If anything, it demands access to each and every area of our lives. Including our work.

I'll never forget my first day back at work after committing myself fully to God's agenda. I felt like the unstoppable force meeting the immovable object. Despite my fresh conviction to go public with my faith, I could sense the inevitable collision with the world that didn't care to hear my views.

In situations like that, it's tempting to force the issue. Since God is bigger than the world, we conclude that His agenda should take priority over all else. As a result, our techniques are often less than tactful.

Needless to say, Jesus wasn't like that. Despite being Lord of all, He entered the world quietly—born to a young woman in an obscure corner of a barn. He never forced Himself on anyone. He just went about His business and let the contrast of those two worlds run their course. And along the way, He was never afraid to be Himself.

Jesus rarely calls us away from what we do professionally. We don't have to quit our jobs. He just calls us to do them from the perspective of who we are in Christ. And as we'll see in the pages that follow, that's when the environment is right for making a difference and making disciples.

ONE MORE WORD ABOUT PURPOSE

Purpose—*why we do what we do*—is the common denominator that pulls these two worlds together. Other than my faith in Christ and the friends who have walked with me through these years, nothing has been more useful to me than my life-purpose statement. Here's how I developed it.

Soon after my backyard resolution with God, a friend gave me some sermon tapes by a preacher named Charles Stanley, whose church was in downtown Atlanta. The tapes were awesome, so I decided to go and see this guy for myself. After fighting through a full parking lot and settling into a seat behind a television-camera platform, I discovered the church had a guest speaker that Sunday...Ronald Blue, C.P.A.

I had gone through all this to hear a bean counter? I almost left, but I'm glad I didn't.

When Ron walked up to the podium, he asked this question, "Suppose your life is a dollar—what are you spending it on?" The question entranced me. How could I have lived thirty-three years and never given a minute's consideration to what I was doing with my life?

"Suppose your life is a dollar—what are you spending it on?"

Before I could get through that thought, Ron stated his life purpose: "I exist to glorify God by using my financial knowledge and experience to help people to become better stewards of the resources that God has given them."

He was the first person that I had ever known who knew why he existed.

I was hooked. I immediately started thinking about my purpose. What could a sales and marketing guy like me do that would glorify God? Salespeople are not usually thought to be paragons of ethics and integrity. How on earth could God use my sales and marketing knowledge and experience?

The next morning I called Ron Blue's office, and through a series of connections and conversations, I came up with a life-purpose statement:

"I, Regi Campbell, exist to glorify God by teaching biblical principles to sales and marketing executives."

When I took up the mantle of leadership in the start-up company, I modified my life-purpose statement to read "to teach, *model, and demonstrate* Christ and His principles in the sales and marketing workplace."

After reading Kevin McCarthy's book, *The On-Purpose Person*, I got even more specific about my purpose. I live "to glorify God by loving, serving, and challenging others to be all they can be, and to give all of themselves to Jesus Christ."

This is what I am attempting to do in every venue of my life every day. I approach work from two perspectives at the same time:

- How can I do my job and do it well?
- How can I make a difference for Christ in the lives of the people I will meet today?

These two drivers *must* work together. Committed Christians who are lousy workers have little influence. And great workers whose faith in Christ is always kept secret have little value in building God's kingdom.

Every day, we have two jobs. We are to be great employees, managers, and business owners. We have to do the jobs that we have to the best of our abilities.

But our other job is to be a secret (or not so secret) agent for God. We are to look at our coworkers, subordinates, clients, superiors, vendors, and owners through the lens that God looks through, and then to love, serve, and challenge them to move toward Christ, one step at a time.

Your life-purpose statement may be radically different from mine. Your skills, talent, experience, and interests may be the polar opposite of mine. But the orders we have from the Boss are the same. He gave this one, overarching, universal command to all of His children just before He left to go be with His Dad. He said, "Go and make disciples" (Matthew 28:19).

Now if you've been around church and church people, you've heard that command many times. But what does it really mean? What does God expect me to do? Teach a class? Become an evangelist? Start giving out tracts?

Answering that question is precisely why this book exists.

"YOU'RE TUNED TO WII FM"

Those are the call letters for "What's in it for me?" That's the station we stay tuned to most of the time. What *is* in this for me? What are the benefits and rewards of living on purpose for Christ every day, at home and at work?

First and foremost, *we experience the peace that comes from knowing that we are being obedient.* Knowing that Jesus gave us this one huge command just before He left and that we are obeying it gives us peace.

Remember how it felt when your dad (or mom) would tell you to do something that was hard...and you did it? Eureka! There was this sense of health, of self-worth, of accomplishment that was almost indescribable. The bar was set high, but you made it over. And it was particularly fun if what you did really, really pleased him.

That's how God responds when we "seek first his kingdom

and his righteousness" (Matthew 6:33). He loves it. We are pleasing Him. It makes Him smile.

I picked up a saying years ago: "People feel good about themselves when they do the right thing." When you stop putting off living for God and start doing the right things every day, you will experience a sense of peace and wholeness that you may have experienced only a few times in your life. Knowing that God has a purpose for your being here and that you are fulfilling that purpose is huge. It's invigorating. It's comforting. It helps us rebound from setbacks and disappointments. No matter what else is happening at work, we can be successful each day when we focus on what He would have us do, and just do it.

> No matter what else is happening at work, we can be successful each day when we focus on what He would have us do.

Second, *we don't feel guilty, ever.* Most people who grew up involved in a church got infected with a tremendous amount of guilt. What is good enough? How can I ever be that good? I can never do enough, share enough, pray enough, give enough to please God.

But if you will become a workplace minister and follow the process that I'm going to show you, you can be free from guilt once and for all. You will be doing what Jesus told you to do—you will be making disciples.

Now, you will get off track from time to time. You'll forget about your ministry. You will get so wrapped up in your job or some big project that you'll forget all about your goals to help people at work move one step closer to Christ. And you'll probably feel bad about it. But it will be conviction, not guilt. Guilt comes from the enemy and paralyzes us. Guilt says "You failed. Give up. You're kidding yourself. What were you thinking?"

Conviction comes from the Father and energizes us. Conviction says, "Remember how much I love you. Get going. You can do it. Get back in the game. I am with you always."

Christians who are the "real deal" gain respect. You will become respected as you walk the talk. When you genuinely and sensitively love and serve the people around you, they will come to respect and even admire you. Your reputation will flourish. You will become a person that others listen to and seek advice from.

I believe that God often blesses the business and work endeavors of people who follow Him and attempt to obey His commands. Now, I'm not a fan of the prosperity gospel. You won't hear me preaching, "Make Jesus your choice and get a Rolls-Royce." But I have seen God tremendously bless men and women who are about our Father's business.

Here's how I explain it. God is our perfect Father, right? Well, the perfect Father wants to look down on His kids and bless them. But when He looks down, what are we holding up? Does He see us holding up our best efforts to Him? Or does He see us holding on to our pride, our business reputation, our vanity built on our self-styled success? Does He see us holding on to certain sins? Bad habits?

I want to make it easy for God to bless me. I don't want His vision clouded when He looks down on me and my family. I'm not saying that I can invoke His blessings by my behavior, but I can make sure that I don't put any distractions between Him and me. He won't have to look through a cloud of junk to see my heart. If He blesses, He blesses…that's up to Him. I've done what I'm supposed to do, and that's very peace-giving.

Finally, *we have heavenly rewards to look forward to.* I know that many people cringe at the thought of doing good stuff on earth so they can get big rewards in heaven. But Scripture talks about rewards more than fifty times. God is big on rewards in heaven. They are going to be there. Someone is going to get them.

I often struggle with this idea of receiving rewards because they are always associated with a competition…the winner gets the award, the loser doesn't. But God's rewards will come from His love for us, and from His desire to reward our faithfulness. We will be so grateful that He made all these things possible that we will give them right back to Him out of our gratitude.

So whether you're moved by the peace that comes from obedience, or by being guilt free for the first time in your life, or by receiving rewards in heaven, join the movement. You will have peace as you do the right thing. And as you do the right thing over and over, you will develop godly character and gain more and more respect. Your reputation as a Christ follower will make you a valuable member of the team. Your work and business endeavors might just get blessed, but your eternal endeavor will absolutely be blessed and rewarded.

You have an open offer for a second job. It's an awesome opportunity. It's a vacancy that only you can fill. If you turn it down, the job won't get done.

Will you sign on?

TURNING IT UP A NOTCH

I GREW UP IN THE HOME OF TWO CHRISTIAN PARENTS. The Bible was read every night and grace was repeated before every meal. I was taken to church. In fact, I was taken to church every time there was church.

But by the time I was in third grade, I developed this strange malady that caused me to get sick every Sunday night, just about the time church was to begin. That was also the time that *The Twentieth Century* with Walter Cronkite came on TV, followed by *The Ed Sullivan Show*. Even after I was saved and baptized at age ten, Arcadia Baptist Church was no match for Elvis Presley, the Beatles, and the Rolling Stones live on television.

So while I did really believe that Jesus was God's Son, that He did really die on the cross for my sins and come back to life, it didn't make much difference to me. After all, my list of sins wasn't all that long. I believed, as every kid does, that I was invincible and that death was forever away from me.

So I settled into a pattern that went like this: I go to church on Sunday, I pray over my food and when there's a crisis, but otherwise, I live my life the way I want to. That's not to say that I wasn't taught right from wrong. Nor that I was a bad kid who did lots of bad things or got in trouble. Quite the contrary. I did okay in school, always had after-school jobs and thus spending money, and I never got in trouble at school or with the law. But there was no meaningful connection between the Christian faith that I was a part of and the life that I lived. I looked no different from every other kid my age, and that remained true through high school and college.

When I graduated from college and was selected for an elite management training program at AT&T, my faith faded even further into the background. Smart, aggressive, hardworking, knowledgeable...those were the adjectives that described success. Being a Christian was okay, but being perceived as "too Christian" was a liability.

So the work environment reinforced my passive Christianity. I can believe what I want, so long as I don't call attention to myself...and so long as I don't create any tension with anyone else about what I believe.

I had joined the silent majority.

PASSIVE VS. ACTIVE CHRISTIANITY

You see, the groundwork was laid early for me to become a passive Christian. I believed, and I never stopped believing, even when I had wandered so far from Christianity that I was like a lost Easter egg in tall grass on Monday morning. But believing was irrelevant to my life every day. The training given me by my parents and teachers guided my behavior, but my faith was something I rarely thought about.

Of the more than six billion people on the earth, two billion declare themselves to be Christians.[1] I believe the majority of these, regardless of their brand (denomination), are passive Christians.

You may fall into that category as well, doing what I did for years. You attend church and take your kids whether they want to go or not. You pray over your food. You're a good person who does the right thing most of the time. And you're going to heaven when you die.

But you may also be ready for a change. You're ready to move from passive to active. You want to do more than sit and soak on Sunday morning. You're tired of having this compartmentalized life where you're afraid of being too secular on Sunday and afraid of being too spiritual the rest of the week. You want to be one person, live one life, and make it matter. You're ready to become an active Christian.

So what is an *active* Christian?

An *active* Christian connects what he does every day with his faith. He has purpose in his life and he lives with intentionality. He is motivated by gratitude, and his life is fulfilling every day and to the very end.

An active Christian connects what he does every day with his faith.

Now that's a mouthful, but becoming an active Christian is a prerequisite if this book is to be meaningful and useful to you.

One of my favorite sayings is, "You can't steer a parked car." So becoming an active Christian requires action, requires movement, requires change.

Two big factors have to be in place before you can become an active Christian and be about our Father's business. You have to know who He is and be motivated to serve Him.

YOUR RELATIONSHIP WITH CHRIST

It was April 1983. I was tying my basketball shoes and getting ready to run out to the gym. The doorbell rang.

"Hi, there. You folks visited our church last Sunday and we thought we'd drop by and say hello."

There were three of them. What could I say?

"Come on in, I guess," I said, a little miffed at a surprise visit without an appointment or so much as a phone call warning. "My wife can visit with you. I'm late for a basketball game."

I headed for the door.

"Mr. Campbell?" the young man said in a halting tone. "Before you go, could I ask you just one question? If you died tonight, where would you spend eternity?"

"Listen, I've been a Christian since I was ten years old," I replied in a not-so-kind voice. "I've taught Sunday school and even started a class once. So don't you worry about me!" I hustled out, shut the door solidly behind me (that means I slammed it), and drove off.

As I was speeding down Providence Road, that little unmistakable voice said, *Regi, if you're so sure, why are you so upset?*

That little encounter was the first of three significant

encounters that led me from being a passive Christian to being an active one.

What I know now, for sure, is that I am a Christian…and that I was a Christian from an early age. As my pastor puts it, it's all in four words contained in John 3:16.

For God so loved the world…

God created the world and me. He loves me. He created me to be one of His most wonderful creations and one of His intimate companions. But just like in our other human relationships, intimacy can't be forced; it must be chosen. Through my DNA, which goes all the way back to Adam, I was born bent away from God. It's like a stamp on my spiritual birth certificate, a permanent mark that says, "This child is a descendant of Adam." Without some intervention, I am inheriting the family debt of sin, not to mention that I'm going to add to the tab with my own behavior.

That He gave…

God gave His Son, Jesus Christ, to die as payment for all of my sins, past, present, and future. He cancels the mark on my birth certificate: "Debts canceled." The debts are changed from my account to His and His account is paid in full. God's free gift of Christ paying it all on the cross removed all the charges from my account.

That whoever believes in Him…

God simply requires that we believe in Jesus Christ: that He is who He says He is and that He did what the Bible says He did. (Came, died, and came back to life.) Dying and coming back to life gives all of His teachings ultimate credibility. No other person has ever done that.

Shall have (receive) eternal life.

When I came to believe in Jesus Christ, God immediately adopted me into His family. I can never be unadopted and neither can you.

So that's it—God *loved*, God *gave*, we *believe*, and we *receive*.

If you have been confused about what being a Christian involves, or you have never told God that you believe in Jesus Christ, stop right now and do it. Just talk to Him and tell Him what you're thinking and feeling. He will hear you, He will accept you, and you will begin a new life and an adventure that will never end.

Let's not get hung up on anything other than the essence. Augustine (354–430 A.D.) is widely thought to have said: "In essentials, unity. In nonessentials, liberty. But in all things, charity." If my John 3:16 gospel isn't the complete picture of salvation for you, don't check out on me. Let's work together with that essential and go where God leads you with the rest of Christian doctrine. Every Christian believes that a relationship with God begins with the truths in John 3:16, so let's not let the enemy get us distracted with nonessentials or what doctrine comes after loved, gave, believe, and receive.

GRATITUDE IS THE MOTIVATOR

In the pages that follow, I'm going to challenge you to be a full-time, on-purpose Christ follower at work, at home, at your kid's soccer game, even in rush-hour traffic when the maniac in the sports car cuts you off.

But you have to be motivated. You have to want to. What makes us want to do things, particularly a thing as scary as being an active, public Christian at work?

I was taught early in my career that there are two motivators of human behavior: fear and desire.

There are two motivators of human behavior: fear and desire.

If we are motivated by *fear*, we will do whatever it takes to relieve the fear. For example, if someone becomes seriously afraid of dying, he may disinfect everything in his house, take flu shots, load up on vitamins, and avoid flying on airplanes. Assuming that he is sane, he will come to a point where the fear subsides enough that he can carry on with life.

Desire is also a powerful motivator. A lot of people are motivated by their desire to please others. Most of us seem to evolve from our childhood with low self-esteem, holding on to a deep desire to gain the approval of our parents and of other people. We will work hard to gain titles, status, and the economic success that symbolize that we are good enough. And some of us make that a lifelong pursuit, committing our lives to a never-ending search to have more and more. We spend our lives stating our worthiness to an unknown audience.

The desire for success is the most visible motivator in the work culture today. We all drive to achieve, to be successful. We want to provide well for our families, no doubt, and we enjoy the recognition that comes from winning. From our bounty, we will be generous with those who are less fortunate. But the drive for success is pretty selfish at its heart. It's about me, me, me.

The forefathers of modern psychology line up behind these

two powerful motivators. And while fear and desire are undeniable motivators for selfish survival and self-actualization, they provide no motivation to do anything selfless, which is what Christianity is all about.

Guilt is also a powerful motivator. We feel bad about something we've done, so we do something good for another person to make ourselves feel better. Or we feel guilty because we are so much better off than someone else. When we see pictures of poor kids in some third world country, we feel guilty about our abundance. We write a check and put it in the mail. We feel better about ourselves as the guilt eases off. As soon as we have done enough good to bring our emotions back to equilibrium, we continue our lives as before.

Compassion is another one. We hurt for the hurting, so we take some action. We write a card, visit the hospital, or send some flowers—all good things. But once we have done enough to make us feel okay about ourselves, we go back to our normal routines. It's human nature.

Generosity will sometimes overtake us. When we are blessed with sudden abundance, we just have to share it with others. When we sold our first company, nothing could prevent me from buying my dad a new car. He hadn't had a new car since he retired, and I knew how much he loved that new-car smell. He loved the big red bow; I loved the giddy feeling I had giving him such a great gift. But as soon as the car got banged up in a rear-ender and he had his first mechanical problem, those feelings were over. I went back to work. He was now driving a newer used car.

So what is the long-term motivator with staying power?

I believe that the only sustainable motivation for selfless behavior is *gratitude*.

Let me say that again a different way. *Only gratitude motivates us to care about others over the long term.* Other emotions will motivate us for a little while, but they won't motivate us for the long pull. And making disciples is a long-term process that requires selfless action over a long period of time.

Only gratitude motivates us to care about others over the long term.

So if gratitude is it, then let's explore three major sources of gratitude. There may be others, but let's talk about the big three that are central to the Christian.

1. Gratitude for forgiveness

For those of us who either came to faith later in life or who drifted away from God for a while, there is a tremendous gratitude for God's forgiveness. We remember the things we did, the lies we told, the selfishness we demonstrated. We remember ourselves as people that we wouldn't like very much today. When we reflect on the fact that God forgave us for all that, that He wiped the slate clean, that He "will remember [our] sins no more" (Hebrews 8:12), we are overcome with gratitude. It's a reference point that we go back to over and over again. In His book, He wiped it clean and it's as if it never happened. He let me start over. That is an amazing, sustaining source of gratitude.

Imagine that you had lived a financially reckless life, running up hundreds of thousands of dollars in debt, making horrible decision after horrible decision. Then one day, you are forced to go to the banker with your hat in your hand, broke and broken, out of options. The banker, to your complete surprise, says, "Your debts are forgiven. I want you to have a great life. Start over, and don't make the same mistakes next time." How grateful would you be to that banker? How often would you remember his incredible kindness to you?

2. Gratitude for blessings and protection

We have so, so much to be thankful for. In America, our prosperity is incredible. The standard of living for people considered poor in the U.S. is far better than the middle class in many parts of the world. And as I have visited with Christians in third world countries, I have been consistently amazed at how grateful these people can be for so little.

I can't get over the blessings that God has given me, and I hope I never do. I have a beautiful, forgiving wife, two great kids who chose great spouses, and good health. It could have been so different if I had gotten what I deserved. But for some reason, known only to my heavenly Father, He chose to bless me.

In 1998, my son Ross was driving home from school for a short weekend. Suddenly, his SUV blew a tire. It swerved and flipped several times, landing wheels down facing the opposite direction on the interstate. Ross was unconscious.

The ambulance attendants apparently used drugs to restart his heart. He was airlifted to a trauma center in downtown Atlanta. He had a closed head injury and was in a coma. His life hung in the balance. The neurosurgeons contemplated doing brain surgery to relieve the pressure inside his skull. That surgery would have unknown but permanent consequences. We prayed. We waited.

About eighteen hours later, following the prayers of literally thousands of people in our church and others, the swelling miraculously stopped and started to abate. My son was saved; his functioning returned to normal, and three months later he was back in medical school. Every day, I remember how God protected my son...how He gave him back to us...how it could have turned out so differently.

I can never pay God back for that blessing. I couldn't even begin to try. But every day, I feel gratitude for His blessings. And that gratitude motivates me to thank Him, to worship Him, to try and please Him with my behavior, and to do everything I know to get other people in on the life He has to offer.

3. Gratitude for the Cross

Some people just seem to get it when it comes to understanding God's love for them. It has to be a supernatural thing.

I have a friend who is one of those people. He pastors one of the largest, most successful churches in metro Atlanta. He was raised in a great home by great Christian parents. He fell in love with God as a teenager. I don't think he has ever strayed five degrees from true north. I am convinced that the biggest sin he ever committed was a speeding ticket. His life has been a truly blessed existence—a great family, a great church life, and a great business career before being led to seminary and full-time ministry.

And now he's making a huge impact for God leading a successful megachurch. The guy just gets it.

I have heard my friend speak to thousands of people about the way God loves us, and he chokes up. It didn't take forgiveness from onerous sin or incredible blessings or protection from disaster for him. God just had a plan to use him in a powerful way, so He gave him a clear understanding of His love from an early age.

Are you ready to turn it up a notch? Do you have a clear understanding of the Good News? Are you ready to start exporting your faith and making disciples?

If you are motivated to take your faith to work by anything other than gratitude, spend some time reflecting on the blessings God has given you. Your salvation, your life, the years you've been given, the relationships He has put in your life…there is plenty of evidence of His love in your life. And I know that there is also pain, death, tragedy, and loss in your life. Everyone has some of that as well. But you will have to focus on the blessings and give God the credit if you are to begin living a life filled with and motivated by gratitude.

> Spend some time reflecting on the blessings God has given you.

Do this right now. Make a list of the things you are grateful for—special people, special experiences, material blessings, unique protections that He has provided, forgiveness for your failures, your salvation, your adoption into His family, His volunteering to be your perfect Father. Keep adding to the list as long as it keeps coming.

Now put that list where you will remember to look at it from time to time…in your day planner, in your Bible, in your journal, or even make it your screen saver.

I believe that the grateful heart is the inexhaustible fuel cell for becoming a workplace minister.

We've got our message; we have our motivation. Now let's develop our method.

RELATIONSHIPS ARE THE "ONE THING"!

WHEN BILLY CRYSTAL LOOKED UP AT JACK PALANCE IN THE movie *City Slickers* and asked about the meaning of life, Curly told him, "It's just one thing." Neither the actor nor the writer who penned that line had any idea how profound or how accurate it was.

Life is about just one thing. It's about relationships.

Life is about relationships.

Now I realize that's a dogmatic statement, but it's true. There are really two relationships that are at the pinnacle of meaning for us humans: our relationship with God and our relationships with people. Let me explain.

Human beings were created for relationships. That's why we were put here in the first place. We are God's highest and best creation, and He made us in His image so that we could have a relationship with Him. Through our belief in Christ, that relationship with God, which was broken because of sin, has been restored. We can take as much or as little advantage of it as we choose, but it's there.

My relationship with God is a little like my relationship with my best friend, Tut Smith. We can talk everyday or not talk for a long time, but I know he is there. I know he loves me. I know that I can call on him for anything. We can use tough words of challenge and soft words of encouragement. It's safe to say exactly how we feel, because we know that we love each other. If I ignore Tut, I'm the one who loses. I miss out on his encouragement, his affirmation, and the love that I feel from him when we talk.

Same with God. The more I call on Him, the more time I spend with Him, the more I love Him and learn from Him and want to be as good for Him as He is for me.

Everything else in life that matters centers around relationships with people.

How can I say that?

From the earliest days of the human race, people needed other people to be happy. "It's not good for the man to be alone," God said of Adam before He created Eve. Today, the most onerous form of punishment in our prison system is solitary confinement. Like them or not, we need people...we need relationships.

There is another, maybe even bigger reason that relationships are that "just one thing."

People are the only things that will go on from this life to the next. Every person will spend eternity somewhere. Stuff will go away...rust, rot, burn, whatever. But people will always exist. Each person will retain his identity, his personality, and his soul somewhere, forever. It's daunting, but it's true. And Jesus coming back to life proved that it's true. A dead man (undoubtedly dead via crucifixion) came back to life. He still had his personality. He had the same appearance. He was the same soul, Jesus of Nazareth, alive, dead...then alive again.

Each of us will live for some number of years. Then we are going to die, and then we are going to wake up somewhere else to live forever, either in the presence of God or apart from Him. There won't be any coming back here, no other interim stops. It's a ticket to one destination. No transfers or round-trips.

You see, seeking first His kingdom is about building relationships with individuals for the purpose of leading them to Christ and then to excellence in walking with Him. It's about being on purpose with every person that God points you to in your work life. And you can start that process today by making an intentionality map of your workplace. Let me explain.

CREATING AN IMAP OF YOUR WORKPLACE

Maps tell us where things are and they help us to get from one place to another, one road, one turn, one step at a time. The intentionality map (or IMAP for short) is a simple tool that I developed several years ago to help me figure out where people in my workplace are spiritually. I added the word *intentionality* to remind me that I need to be intentional in everything that I do in these relationships, with the overarching goal of helping them move one step at a time toward an excelling relationship with Christ. But just like driving through a city with a map in your hand, it's one turn, one red light, then a green one…then another turn. Sometimes, you even have to back up because you weren't where you thought you were. It's just the nature of moving from one place to another when you haven't been there before.

And so it is when you embark on the spiritual journey with someone. They have never been there before, and their journey is different from yours and from anyone else's as well. The IMAP is a starting point, a "best guess" as to where a coworker is spiritually. The columns on the IMAP show the columns that Christ would have all of us travel, ending up as excelling followers who are investing in others to help them find their way to Him.

And if you're like me, drawing your IMAP could be the thing that opens your eyes to the true state of affairs around you. When I first committed my life to Christ, the office used to overwhelm me. As I described before, I felt like the only Christian in the world taking on an office full of hostile unbelievers. Had I known how to analyze my situation, I might have been a lot smarter in my approach. Looking back, there were a lot more allies than I realized. There were also a lot fewer hostiles than I thought. And, of course, there were all kinds of people in between.

The IMAP is just what it says—it's a quick picture, not a movie. *It's not a judgment; it's a first impression based on observation.* The IMAP is a model that can be applied to virtually any work environment. It simply suggests that everyone falls into one of five categories or spiritual profiles. No matter where you go, you can be fairly certain you will find these five types of people. It's not intended to be judgmental; it's to get a survey of the landscape before you plan your strategy. Based on the IMAP, you can develop a unique game plan to point people toward a relationship with God.

Here's how I do it. I simply draw a chart with five columns. And under each of those columns, I list the names of everybody in the organization that is within my sphere of influence. The IMAP below shows the headings of the categories.

A	B	C	D	E
APATHETIC Don't know/don't care about spiritual things.	**BEGINNING TO SEARCH** Don't know the answers, but beginning to think there might be something there.	**CONFESSING** Believes that Jesus Christ was God, etc. but you would never know it.	**DEVELOPING** Seriously commited to Christianity and is pursuing God. Not ashamed of their faith.	**EXCELLING** Living out the Christian Life and trying to help others get there. Sold out!

Sphere of Influence

Column A is for **Apathetic**. When it comes to religion or spiritual things, this is where ignorance meets apathy. People in this column don't know and they don't care. These are people who do not know Jesus Christ and have no interest in spiritual things, though they may have had a religious experience sometime in the past. They may even express resentment toward Christians or God.

Column B is **Beginning**. These are people who are beginning to seek and search. While they do not believe in Jesus Christ, they are beginning to show interest in spiritual things, whether it's reading books, listening to tapes, or attending a church. They may not own a Bible, but they might have a library of books such as *The Celestine Prophesy* and *The Da Vinci Code*. They may read the horoscopes every day and talk often about God, but they don't have the answers and may or may not be conscious of their search for truth.

Column C is **Confessing** or **Christian**. These are people who say "I believe." They have some affiliation with a church or they may attend mass. At the same time, there isn't evidence of growth in their lives. They may still be harboring sinful behaviors and not exhibit any of the fruit of the Spirit. They probably make little or no reference to their faith at work. They are the silent majority, the chosen frozen. If there were a public trial where they were charged with being a follower of Jesus Christ, there would not be enough evidence to convict them. These are passive Christians.

Column D is **Developing**. These are people who are *doing* something to grow in their Christian faith. They are in a Bible study or small group. They read the Bible and Christian books. They pray. They listen to sermons or talks, and they are growing in their faith. You can see peace, love, joy, patience, kindness, goodness, faithfulness, gentleness, and self-control in their lives. They are most likely involved in a church or other ministry activities. They are active followers of Jesus Christ and are not ashamed to be so.

Column E is **Excelling**. The distinguishing characteristic of an excelling person is that he takes *intentional action to bring others* to a growing faith in Christ. These people understand and embrace the mission of making disciples. They exhibit the same attributes as someone in column D, but in addition, they are actively involved in leading others to next steps in their walk with Christ. They lead small groups; they teach, mentor, coach, and disciple others.

WHAT'S A SPHERE OF INFLUENCE?

Who do you come into regular contact with? Who do you care about? Who has God put on your radar screen? Who do you have some connection to?

Who has God put on your radar screen?

These are the people within your sphere of influence. Their names will easily flow out of your mind and onto your IMAP worksheet. Names that just happen to be in the company directory or customer names on a list aren't necessarily people in your sphere of influence.

Here's a cool way to come up with your list.

Think up—Who are the people that you *work for*? Your boss. His or her boss. Managers. Executives. Board members. Owners. Think of the people that are over you in your workplace who you have some connection or relationship with. Think about former bosses that you keep in contact with, as well as current ones.

Think down—Who are the people that *work for you*? Your subordinates. Their subordinates. People who are at lower-level jobs in other parts of the organization. Again, think of the names of people that you have a relationship with. God may have connected you just for this moment and purpose. Remember former employees, too.

Think in—Who are the people who *serve you*? You are their client or customer. This includes vendors, service providers, consultants, and professionals. These are people who call on you and provide services to your organization, either now or in the past.

Think out—Who are the people that *you serve*? These are your organization's current and former clients, prospects, and customers. Who have you connected with out there in the marketplace?

Think across—Who are the people that you *work with*? This is probably your biggest group. These are peers, colleagues, and professional friends in your network. These are people you see as your equals. They are on the same level as you, the same footing. You can talk to them about spiritual things without even thinking about being fired or being sued…and you can do it with a smaller lump in your throat.

Now, how do we know where to write the names?

Think about each person one at a time and ask God to help you remember what you have heard and observed in your interactions with that person. Here are some questions to stimulate your thinking:

What has this person said? Think back to conversations you've had with this person. Did she say anything that gave you a clue about her religion or her opinion about religion? Have you noticed her reaction to you or other Christians when topics like church, Christianity, God, or Jesus have come up?

One approach that has been effective for me is to make small references to my faith and then watch and listen for the person's reaction. This is called raising "faith flags" and it is detailed by William Carr Peel and Walt Larimore in their book *Going Public with Your Faith.*

> Faith flags are about identity. Just as a flag helps you recognize the nationality of a ship, faith flags help a person recognize you as someone to whom faith, the Bible, prayer, and God is important.... A "faith flag" looks for, but doesn't demand a response. When you raise a faith flag, you'll be able to watch for a person's verbal and non-verbal responses and gauge interest in a non-threatening way.[2]

Listening and watching how people respond to you and to the faith flags that you raise will help you make a "first guess" about where to place them on your IMAP.

What have you seen? What people decorate their workspaces and offices with often tells you what they care about. What plaques or quotations does he display? What pictures or symbols do you see on his desk? What books are around?

Where does this person go? When she talks about the places she goes for fun, where does she go? Where does she take her family? What kind of vacations does she take? Do spiritual things ever influence where she hangs out (or, more importantly, where she doesn't) or the activities that she's involved in?

Who are this person's heroes? Who does this person look up to or idolize? When he talks about people he admires, who does he name and why?

How does this person behave? Does this person use horrible language that shows disrespect for God? What does her attitude tell you about her? Is she peaceful or struggling? If she's peaceful, has she ever said anything that gave you a clue about the source of that peace? Does she get involved in activities of compassion? Does she demonstrate a caring attitude toward others? Is she selfish or selfless?

What is this person's reputation? How do others feel about him? Is he looked up to and respected, or ignored and tolerated? What are his work habits and standards? Is he known as honest or dishonest?

For years, I've been told that Christians can't be judges, but they can inspect fruit. Unfortunately, many Christians have inspected the fruit so they could decide who to avoid. We want to be with the strong believers; they make it easy. They agree with what we believe, praise us for our good works, and pray for us.

We would rather avoid the people who don't believe as we do. They make us uncomfortable. They might ask questions that we don't know the answers to. They might even be a bad influence on us; we might become like them, we think. And we do have to be careful, as the Bible warns that "bad company corrupts good character" (1 Corinthians 15:33). But we don't have to enter into their behavior. We can love and accept without participation. Sure, it's going to feel uncomfortable, but if we don't invest in these people, who will? Granted, we're more comfortable hanging out with our own. After all, "birds of a feather..." right? But that's not what Jesus did, and He wants us to emulate Him.

The question is, will we be about our Father's business in our work relationships, or will we just do what we have to do to make a living and enjoy life? Will we have intentionality in our actions? Will we think about how we might influence that person to move toward the next step, the next column?

If we're going to be like Jesus, we're going to meet the people in our sphere of influence right where they are and love them just as they are. Our IMAP gives us a starting point so we can recognize what obstacles lie ahead and develop some strategies for our relationships.

If we're going to be like Jesus, we're going to meet the people in our sphere of influence right where they are and love them just as they are.

For me, having a general idea of where everybody stands feels like finally getting my garage organized. Suddenly, I know what I have to work with, as well as what needs the most work. I go from being overwhelmed by an office of hostile persecutors to having a clear idea of how to approach my mission of sharing Christ in the workplace. Now it's simply a matter of developing strategies to help these people move from one column to the next.

Before we go any further, I want you to get on the Internet and go to www.amfb.com, register on the site, and then click on the button that says "Create your IMAP." You can create your IMAP and print it out neatly; and you can easily update it as people in your sphere of influence take "next steps" and move from column to column toward "excelling." If you're not into technology just yet, then take out a sheet of paper and sketch out the IMAP of your workplace into these five columns. Refer to the chart on the page earlier in this chapter if you need a reminder about the columns. Can you think of two or three coworkers who don't care at all about spiritual things? Put their names in column A. Can you think of two or three colleagues who are searching but aren't believers (Column B's)? List the people who say "Oh, I believe," who have all kinds of potential, but who are silent and passive about their faith. Put their names in column C. Can you identify the growing, involved active Christians that you work with? Put them in column D. Can you identify one or two people who want to see others become Christians and who might be willing to consider joining with you on your mission? List their names in column E.

You're moving! If all you ever do is systematically and genuinely pray for these people to move column by column toward God, then you've contributed invaluably to their lives and to their journeys. But there will be more. God will lead you to love these people—to serve them and to involve yourself in their lives to help them become excelling disciples.

Jesus was strategic in His methods of making disciples. And good strategy has made all the difference in the world in my attempts to be an influence for Christ in the marketplace. I long for you to discover the freedom and fulfillment of using this practical way to work for Christ as you work for a living.

Let me say one thing about one big word: *intentionality*. I connect the word *active* into the word *intentional*. Let me illustrate what I mean.

Since I was fifteen years old, I have played *with* the game of golf. I've never been very good at it, but I always wanted to be. I've bought new clubs, taken lessons, and taken up the game three different times. I have also given up on the game and sold those clubs in garage sales three different times.

You could say that I have been an *active* golfer from time to time. But my purpose in playing golf was to enjoy the game and get good enough that I would not embarrass myself or my playing partners.

Kevin did some contract work for my first company. I found out that Kevin, whom I listed as an Apathetic A on my IMAP grid, was an avid golfer. I had never talked with Kevin about spiritual things, but I had observed that he was a heavy smoker who seemed to always be uptight. He was constantly faced with either not enough business or too much business; all of it with unattainable customer deadlines.

I knew I would have to earn his trust if I was going to ever earn the right to ask him about his views on God. I figured that golf was the only thing we had in common, so I started playing golf with him. My purpose in golfing was now twofold: to enjoy the game *and* to find out what Kevin believed. My goal was to verify my guess that Kevin was an Apathetic A and to get ideas on how I might stimulate him to begin a search for truth…to become a B who is beginning to seek. (More about Kevin later.)

I knew I would have to earn his trust if I was going to ever earn the right
to ask him about his views on God.

That's *intentionality*. It's doing what you would do anyway,
but doing it with a kingdom purpose as well as an earthly purpose.

And that's what we're going to be talking about for the rest
of this book. What can we do to move the people in our sphere
of influence from column to column in our IMAP? How can we
move them toward excelling in Christ one column, one step at
a time?

THE APATHETIC

"Don't Know and Don't Care"

LET'S START OUR JOURNEY THROUGH THE FIVE-COLUMN IMAP grid with the Apathetic A's—the people we work with who show no interest in spiritual things.

One caution here: neither you nor I will ever know the true state of another person's heart, so our impression of someone as being spiritually apathetic has a high risk of being wrong. No matter how close we get, no matter how intimate our friendship, only God Himself knows the heart of a person. So it's super important that we don't get carried away trying to judge the people in our sphere of influence so we can label them and put them accurately into our grid. The IMAP is just a first impression, a quick assessment based on conversations that you've had, behavior that you've observed, and things you've heard them say.

Apathetic A's are people who don't know and don't care about Christianity. They may know a lot about God; they may have even been heavy-duty into religion at some point in their lives. But for whatever reason, they have now come to a place where spiritual things just don't matter to them. They have no felt need for a higher power. As one young man told a friend recently, "I just don't need God right now."

Only God Himself knows the heart of a person.

In reality, doesn't that describe most of the people that we work with? Isn't that the prevalent attitude of the people at the office? Sure, there are plenty of exceptions, even offices and factories where religious people outnumber the apathetics. But by and large, we live in a secular society and many if not most people have no felt need for God day to day.

Here is one of the most important points in this book: Until we know better, *we should treat everyone as if they are Apathetic A's.*

Remember, our goal is to motivate Apathetic A's to begin an *active* search into spiritual things. We're not trying to lead them to the Lord...at least not directly. We are interested in helping them take the next step. That's it. If we can inspire them to start to look for answers, then we can count on God to draw them to Himself and lead them to the Truth.

Which brings us to the next big question: How *do* we respond to an apathetic person? What can we do to stimulate an interest in spiritual things? How can God use us to stir that person's heart, to shake him from his lethargy and inspire him to begin a search for truth?

IT ALL STARTS WITH LOVE

So, if most of the people we work with seem apathetic, and if we are to treat everyone as if they are apathetic until we learn more, what's the first thing we must do?

We have to love the people we work with.

We have to love the people we work with.

Christ directed us to. He told us to "love your neighbor as yourself" (Matthew 22:39). He wants you to love the people you work with, even those you don't particularly like. You cannot minister to someone that you don't love. And since God is love, He's not going to show up in a relationship where there is no love.

Love is a choice you make. It's a verb, not a noun. Sure, there are those who fall in love, as if love were an accident, a hole that they fell into. But the kind of love I'm talking about here is volitional love, an act of the will. It's deciding that you love someone because God made them, God loves them, and God instructed you to love them, too.

The catalyst for me to begin actively loving people was the discovery of God's unconditional love for me. God just decided that He loved me. I didn't look a certain way, belong to a particular political party, have a particular size or shape...He just chose to love me. I didn't grasp that until age thirty-three, but when I did, my attitude toward other people began to change.

You see, if God chose to love me—just decided to—without me doing anything to deserve it, what right do I have to require anyone else to do something or be something before I love them? Love is an attitude of the heart, and it's an attitude that we can choose to have. It forces us to drop our prejudices, our biases, our stereotypes, and our personal opinions. Love is a choice, and an attitude of love is a choice as well.

So much of our ability to love others stems from our experience. If we have been loved, forgiven, cared for, and made to feel secure, then it's easier for us to give love to others. If we've been hurt, rejected, criticized, and lied to, then we have a harder time giving love.

A speaker I heard once put it this way: "What's down in the well comes up in the bucket." If we have bitterness, anger, resentment, jealousy, and guilt in our hearts (the well), then that is what comes up in the bucket of our words, our behavior, and our attitudes. You can't fake it.

But if your heart is full of love, gratitude, peace, and forgiveness, those qualities will come up in your bucket. And that's what those around you will feel.

How do I get rid of that bitter water in my well? Do I just drop the charges against everyone who has done me wrong? Do I just let go of the stuff that happened to me as a kid? That just lets everyone off the hook. What about justice?

No, it doesn't let everyone off the hook. It just puts their behavior under the jurisdiction of the right Authority. God knows their sins and He is a just God. Let Him handle it. We all understand what *delegation* means. Why not delegate these matters to the Boss? He knows facts that you don't, and He has a plan for those people that you may have no clue about. He will take care of it in time, one way or the other.

We hope that people who have wronged us will find Christ and get the same pardon for their offenses that we got. But if not, then it's between them and Him. I'm not the judge, and more importantly, I'm not the warden who is charged with enforcing the punishment.

The key is to train myself to look at people the way God looks at me. If He chooses to love me, just as I am, then what gives me the right to withhold love from other people, just as they are? He forgave me, so I must forgive them. He loved me before I deserved it; I choose to love them, whether they deserve it or not.

The key is to train myself to look at people the way God looks at me.

Cam Lanier was my business mentor over most of the last twenty years. When we would go into negotiating sessions, attempting to buy different companies, he would always force us to go over our reasons for wanting to make the acquisition. He would always repeat this challenge, "You'd better be honest, because if you aren't, you will 'telegraph' it to the other side."

I can't explain exactly how it works, but we do telegraph our true feelings to people. I have watched conservative, middle-aged businessmen interact with young programmers with their hair in ponytails. Will they be nice to these very important employees? You betcha, because they need their skills. But do their eyes, their gestures, their body language communicate love? Not at all…and the ponytail crowd picks it up every time.

I have watched young managers run meetings with beautiful young female execs and more mature, less beautiful females. The male managers telegraph totally different messages—one of acceptance and one of rejection. If you're that young manager and the less beautiful person is an Apathetic A, the door for having influence for Christ is slammed shut in that moment.

So your homework assignment for today is really a heart-work assignment. Take a moment right now and ask God to clear your heart of any resentment that you have for someone at work, especially those that you listed on your IMAP. Ask Him to relieve you of the hurt feelings you're holding on to because of someone's careless words; of that jealousy that you've felt for your colleague who's been playing the one-upmanship game. Ask God to clear the clutter from your relationships and to give you a new capacity to love those around you.

ACCEPTANCE IS A DIFFERENT THING

I believe that it is possible to love someone and not accept them, just like we can accept someone and not love them (which I call tolerance). We won't gain influence with someone through tolerance. We have to love them *and* accept them *and communicate* that we do both.

You see, people gravitate toward environments of acceptance and they avoid environments of rejection. If someone senses rejection from you, they will avoid being around you. They won't see the good things that you do, and they will ignore the things that you say. Your influence with them will be nil.

But if they sense your acceptance, they will listen to you. They will watch your life. They will want to be around you, and if you are consistently living out the Christian life, they will be drawn to that life.

Imagine a dial like the volume control on your stereo. Call it your acceptance dial. When you are around people that are like you, accepting them is easy. Your dial doesn't even have to move. It can be comfortably set on 2 or 3. When you encounter that squeaky-voiced person from accounting, you need to turn your acceptance dial up to 5 or 6, because she just naturally gets on your nerves. And when you run into the guy from operations who is covered in tattoos and who clearly does not like you, your dial needs to get spun all the way around to 10…and fast.

Now practice dialing up your acceptance *before* you encounter people other than your close friends and colleagues. Be intentional. Remember that you are on a mission to have influence for Jesus Christ and to help people move toward Him one step at a time.

Remember that God made them, just like He made you. He gave that person that squeaky voice. He gave the operations guy the freedom to get those tattoos. He has a plan for their lives just as He has one for yours. They just need to find Him, and you have a key role in helping them do that.

Ronald Reagan's archenemy in Congress was Tip O'Neill. Tip would stand in front of the press and rail about Reagan, demeaning everything about him from his politics to his personal ethics. Often Reagan would be asked to respond to O'Neill's vicious attacks and accusations. He would reply, "Well, that's just old Tip." There it is. Acceptance. Different politics, different opinions, even personal attacks, yet Reagan accepted O'Neill as a person.

Can you look at the people in your workplace and say "Well, that's just old John" or "Well, that's just old Kathy"? When you do, you start to create an environment of acceptance which lays the groundwork for meaningful relationships and dialogue.

PRAYER LEADS YOU TO PURPOSE

Here are three overarching promises about prayer as it relates to the people in your workplace. These promises have revolutionized my day-to-day existence, and I believe they can do the same for you.

Promise Number 1—Prayer changes your agenda.
Praying for the people on your IMAP grid will give you a kingdom focus each day. Before you start work, put your IMAP in front of you and pray for the people on your grid. You can pick them randomly, pray for the A's one day and the B's the next, or however you choose to approach it. But praying for the people in your sphere of influence every day is a "must do."

Ask, "Lord, which of these people do I need to pray for today?" and then pay attention to the name or names He draws your eye to. Ask, "Father, which of these people do I need to touch today?" Be ready to jot down the name He draws your attention to. Ask, "Lord, what would You have me do for (whomever He has directed your attention to)?"

You see, there's a huge difference between coming up with some grandiose plan for leading someone to Christ and this daily approach. That's what being about my Father's business is all about—getting daily orders and following them. One person, one day, one step at a time.

> Praying for the people in your sphere of influence every day is a "must do."

Over the years of using the IMAP grid, I have yet to approach God this way and have Him not direct me to someone on my list. Sometimes it's just a name that He urges me to pray for. But usually He puts the idea of a phone call, a note, a book or CD to give, or a meal or a cup of coffee to schedule.

When it's all said and done, this is what evangelism and discipleship are about. Daily, relational, intentional, God-led loving on the people in our lives for the purpose of helping them move one step closer to the Savior. It's so simple, yet so true. We ask God for our daily assignment, He gives it to us, and we obey. And guess what? You can still get your work done, you can still excel at your job, and you can still be who you are, doing what you do every day. Only now, you are about your Father's business as you do your own business.

I believe that our faith gets built when we see God answer our prayers. When we ask God something and He answers, that's pretty affirming. After all, He is invisible. As we ask Him to direct us to names on our IMAP grid and He does, we start to see His involvement with our efforts. And when we follow through and do what He puts on our minds to do, we feel great about ourselves. We have received instructions from the God of the universe, and we obeyed. We are making progress.

But the crème de la crème comes when He lets us see the fruit of His work…when He lets us be there when He does something in someone's life because of our obedience.

Early on the morning of March 8, 1999, I was praying for Craig Callaway. Craig seemed to be stuck as a lifelong Beginning to Search B, a skeptical seeker who was never going to get it. But on this morning, these words came to me: "He's just making deals with everyone in his life. He has this 'deal' with you—as long as he keeps 'pursuing truth' by meeting with you, then he can put off taking the 'leap of faith' that is always required to become a believer." Wow!

I wrote down a couple of tough, confrontational questions to ask Craig and then headed off to meet him for our breakfast at the Sunrise Café.

As we waited for our food, Craig was talking about the weekend he had just spent with his parents. His dad, who spent much of his career working with lobbyists in state government, had been describing the ugly underbelly of politics—how everything was negotiated, how it wasn't about truth and commitment, just about making deals. Craig said, "There is no way that I want to live like that, a life defined by one deal after another."

There it was, teed up beautifully. Had to be a God thing.

I said, "But isn't that what you're doing? You've been making deal after deal—with me, with Kerry [his wife], and even with your kids. With me, we read books together; you meet me for breakfast after breakfast, but there is never a real reason for you to continue your 'search.' You know the Truth; you're just afraid to accept it. Your deal with me is, 'I'll keep being interested if you'll keep being interested.' Your deal with Kerry is that she knows the Truth and wants you to find it. So as long as you're 'seeking,' then that trades off for her concern for your finding the Truth. Your girls keep asking 'Our friend Chelsea is Catholic, Daddy. What are we?' Your deal with them is to give them trite answers and avoid taking a real stand. All of your deals allow you to keep treading water, but they aren't taking you anywhere. If you admire truth and commitment, then what holds you back from acknowledging the Truth that will make you a man of character and commitment?"

He paused, looked me straight in the eye, and said, "Nothing."

A few minutes later, we sat in my car and prayed a clumsy prayer together. That day, Craig Callaway crossed over from B to C, from seeker to saved, from deal maker to disciple.

And my faith? It got a huge boost. The idea of Craig making deals with me and the other people close to him had *never* occurred to me before that morning. For God to give me that concept and then to hear him verbalize his disdain for being a deal maker only forty-five minutes later had to be God. And the results—Craig praying to receive Jesus Christ after a twelve-year search—had to be God and God's timing as well. My faith was so strengthened! I had been about ready to give up. But watching what happened that day, I learned that I am never to give up. As long as the Lord keeps a person on my IMAP, and He keeps giving me occasional assignments to pray for or touch that person, then I will keep at it and know that I'm doing what He wants me to do. He is responsible for the outcome; I'm responsible for seeking orders and obeying them.

Promise Number 2—Prayer changes your outlook.
Think back to your childhood. Remember when your dad would give you some assignment to do? Sometimes it would be really easy, but sometimes it would just seem overwhelming or even impossible. But when you did it, when you came through, what a feeling! This man, whom you so wanted to please, gave you a job to do and you did it.

You felt great about yourself. You knew that you pleased him. And for some strange reason, you loved both yourself and him a little more. Maybe it was because he stretched you a little and you sensed his love in that assignment. Maybe it was because your success relieved a little doubt that you had about yourself. Or maybe it was that your success somehow made your dad a little more approachable, a little more connected to you than before.

All of these things come into play when we take daily assignments from our heavenly Father and carry them out successfully.

Our faith is built up when we pray and get answers to our prayers. Our self-confidence is strengthened and we gain a deep sense of fulfillment when we take on an assignment from God and we get it done. All this is made even sweeter by the fact that we aren't responsible for the results. God, in His own time and for His own purposes, will use our obedience to accomplish what He wants to accomplish in our lives and in the lives of those in our sphere of influence.

It's like being a soldier in a battle. We get our assignment and we carry it out. It's not our job to win the war. It's not even our job to win the battle. We are responsible only for doing what we are asked to do at a given moment. Those in authority over us are responsible for the outcomes.

But as we follow orders, as we participate in the battle, we experience a deep sense of belonging—a sense of camaraderie with our fellow soldiers and a deep sense of commitment and loyalty to our Commanding Officer.

Praying for the people in your sphere of influence will change you. You will become more "others" focused. You will start to care about other people's deals and not just your own. You will start to genuinely love people that before you didn't really care for. You won't exactly know how it happened, but you'll find yourself overlooking their bad habits and attributes. You'll start to see them as God saw you—sinful, undeserving, rebellious, ungrateful. Yet those labels won't matter because somehow you'll just love them anyway.

Praying for the people in your sphere of influence will change you.

Earlier I told you about Kevin, my golfing buddy. I hadn't talked to Kevin for a while, so the other day I called him and asked him to lunch. As we ate and talked, it hit me—I'm enjoying this. I've come to enjoy spending time with this guy who does all the things I hate: smokes, swears, and seems to care only about his work and his golf handicap. Prayer had changed me, and I didn't even know it was happening. God has done something in me: to soften me, to make me more patient, more loving, more accepting of Kevin—not just to make me a nicer guy, but to use me in Kevin's life.

Promise Number 3—Prayer changes your environment.
Now this may seem a little out there, but don't blame me. I got it from Scripture and have experienced its truth. The enemy (Satan and his servants) surrounds people who don't yet know Jesus Christ. The unholy trinity of the world, the flesh, and the devil keeps them numbed to the truth of God and to His magnetism.

In Luke 10:5, Jesus instructs the disciples about how to first enter into someone's home. They are to say, "Peace to this house." The word Jesus used for "peace" here is the same word that He used in John 14:27 when He said, "Peace I leave with you; my peace I give you. I do not give to you as the world gives. Do not let your hearts be troubled and do not be afraid."

Jesus is talking about peace that is a God-originated presence.

In his book *Prayer Evangelism*, Ed Silvoso explains that Satan's presence around those who don't know Christ is reinforced when Christians reject them and judge them. But when we pray for them, we replace the spirit of the evil one with the Spirit of God. They become seekers, curious and more open.

"When we speak blessings over those in our circle of influence," Silvoso writes, "sooner or later people who used to avoid us will begin to seek us out, opening the door to fellowship."[3]

Silvoso teaches that we are to speak peace to them, to fellowship with them, to take care of their needs, and to proclaim the Good News...in that order.

Recently, my wife and I and some friends began a small group with several young couples. Two of the couples are not Christians, and one of the guys is an Apathetic A. He has said repeatedly that he isn't interested in God. But with a ton of people praying for him, he accepted the invitation to join the group.

What changed his mind? Why did he say yes to something that he has said no to over and over? I believe that those prayers replaced the demons of doubt that have surrounded him since his early teens with the presence of peace...of God's peace. That freed him up to begin to fellowship with some folks he knows to be Christians. That's a next step, and that's what it's all about.

I believe that praying for people in your sphere of influence can change their environment, regardless of whether they're an

Apathetic A or an Excelling E. God inhabits the prayers of His people. Where the Light is, the darkness can't be. And when we pray God's blessing on people that we care for, the enemy has more trouble causing them trouble than when we fail to pray.

REMEMBER, YOUR GOAL IS "JUST ONE STEP"

Apathetic A's seem to dominate the workplace, outnumbering the rest by a large margin. So as you go about your daily grind, keep praying and following orders. Your goal is not to lead them to Christ. Your goal is to help them to begin a search for truth. There is always an interim step between apathy and commitment, a step where an awareness of God takes root.

Your goal is to help them to begin a search for truth.

These steps are clearly illustrated by two books written by Lee Strobel. *The Case for Faith* starts with the premise that there has to be a God. That takes faith to believe, but Strobel makes a compelling case for having faith in God. Then his other book, *The Case for Christ*, builds on the foundation that there is a God and proves that Jesus Christ was Himself deity. *The Case for Faith*…from A to B. *The Case for Christ*…from B to C. See how it works?

Here's how my intentionality map changes as people take next steps:

INTENTIONALITY MAP

Apathetic	Beginning To Search	Confessing Christian	Developing Disciple	Excelling Christian
Daryl	Bob P.	Doug	Juliet	Andy
Steve	Chuck	Jeff	Paul	Steve
Robert	Craig	Randall	Bob D.	John
Julia	Sam	Dave	Fred	Charlie
	Al	Ken	Tim	Bill
	Steve	Craig		

I have made so many mistakes in trying to lead people to the Lord. I will be in heaven before I find out about all of the opportunities that I missed by not doing or saying something. But the mistakes that I can recall almost always happened because I was trying to go too fast and I skipped important steps.

Once, I had reached out to an employee and her family in a special way, helping her husband find a job and meeting with her son who was going through a challenging time. One day she asked me, "Why are you being so nice to me and my family?" Instead of taking this as a signal to help her move from apathy to beginning to search, I dropped the whole load. I started telling her about Jesus living through me, the exchanged life, stuff that she had no possible context for. She finally said, "Well,

I don't get all that," and cut me off. It was years before we had another meaningful conversation about spiritual things.

So, love…accept…pray…obey…walk the walk…and think one step at a time. Ask God to move your Apathetic A's into a search mode. Ask Him to give them a curiosity about spiritual things. Ask Him to use you in whatever way He chooses to help them take the next step.

BEGINNING TO SEARCH

From Apathy to Active Interest

EVERY NOW AND THEN, THE NEWS WILL FLASH A STORY ABOUT a volcano somewhere in the world that is becoming active. We'll see pictures of the steamy crater as it begins to spew flaming lava and ash. People who live nearby will start to pay attention to the flashes and rumblings as they try to assess how it might affect them. No one is quite sure what is going to happen, but something is, and probably sooner than later.

The people that I put into column B of my intentionality map are like that. They have become active in their search for God. They are reading, asking questions, talking to their workmates about the books they've read or the talks they've heard. They are Beginning to Search B's.

The dividing line between A's and B's isn't belief; it's whether there is activity that has finding answers to spiritual questions as its purpose. B's are actively searching, looking for answers, interested in spiritual things, but not calling themselves Christians.

The opposite of love isn't hate; it's apathy. So when we put a name in column A, we are guessing that person doesn't care about spiritual things right now. He's on the opposite end of the scale from an Excelling E, the person who is in love with God, actively learning and following Him, and attempting to help others find Him.

But unlike an Apathetic A, a Beginning to Search B cares. B's have an interest in finding truth. They may think they have found it. They may be passionate in their conviction that Christianity is *not* it...but there is passion.

Most B's will say they believe in God, but that isn't a defining characteristic of a searcher. A survey by Barna Research showed that 95 percent of Americans say they believe in God, and 85 percent of the population identify themselves as Christians. Yet most of these are either confused or passive in their beliefs. Almost two-thirds have no idea what John 3:16 refers to, according to Barna.[4]

It's unlikely that these folks have an active prayer life, except when there is a life-and-death crisis. There is little involvement with a church. Most don't read the Bible regularly, although some may have several Bibles in the house. If they are Christians (and only God knows if they are), they are dormant, like a bear hibernating through a cold winter.

But B's are active. They are readers. They are thinkers. They are debaters. Many think they have found the answer, and it may be years before they discover that they chose to climb a religious ladder that was leaning against the wrong wall.

Earlier, I said that you can't steer a parked car. Well, B's are moving cars. They are looking for direction. And ultimately they will be steered in some direction, by someone or something.

B's are looking for direction.

B's are interested in spirituality, though they may be turned off by the word *God* and they are certainly going to struggle with the name *Jesus*. But there is a little flame that flickers inside of them...a curiosity, a yearning, a stake in the ground that says "I don't know what it is, but I know there's something or someone out there that's bigger than me—that created this incredible thing called earth and that controls the universe."

The apostle Paul describes this sense of an Almighty in his letter to the Romans. He says that "since the creation of the world God's invisible qualities—his eternal power and divine nature—have been clearly seen, being understood from what has been made, so that men are without excuse" (Romans 1:20).

When this sense that there is an Almighty comes together with a genuine interest in finding answers to spiritual questions, a B is born.

B's may be really mad at God and completely turned off by church, but there continues to be a caring, an interest, a spark inside, even if it's a negative spark. The person that we list as a B cares about God things and, to one degree or another, is searching for something in the spiritual realm.

THE SEARCH BEGINS WITH DISRUPTION

While B's may have a curiosity about spiritual things, it's only when it starts to matter that the curiosity becomes an active search. As the adage goes, "People don't buy solutions to problems they don't have."

You'd have a hard time selling snowballs to Eskimos, and folks who live in the desert don't have much of an appetite for sand. There has to be a gap between what we have and what we need before we start to care. If all of our needs are met, we think we are self-sufficient and autonomous. We may have an intellectual curiosity, but there won't be any urgency to find answers.

But then comes *disruption*.

Some of the most famous words in American spaceflight history are, "Houston, we have a problem." That's disruption.

Something happens that you didn't expect...and it's big. There's a sudden, direct threat to you or to your family. You hear those dreaded words, "There's a lump in your breast." "Your son has been in an accident." "Your father has been taken to the hospital with a heart attack." Your wife looks you in the eye and says, "We have different dreams." Your position at work is being outsourced. The ultrasound shows that the baby may have a problem. The guy you've been dating stops calling. You've been passed over for the promotion again. The hamstring injury is serious, so serious that your days of playing tennis are over, and you're the team's number one player. You've been turned down for the job after the third interview...for the third time in a row.

This is what I call *negative disruption*. Life is going along, and then all of a sudden, some uncontrollable, undeniable, unpleasant thing happens that disrupts it. You are hurled from an even-keel, steady state into trouble mode without warning. When this happens, we swing into action, doing all we can to fix things, to make things go back to steady state, back to control, back to safe.

If the tires on my car are relatively new and working fine, the likelihood of selling me a tire is almost zero. But let me have a blowout with no spare, and I'm a customer. I have a need, and I'll figure out some way to pay for the new tire, almost regardless of how much it costs. That felt need is due to a negative disruption to the status quo.

A huge part of the advertising that we are exposed to is aimed at positioning a product in our minds so that when there is disruption, we think of that product as the solution and we go buy it straightaway. Coke is one of the largest advertisers in the world. Their goal is *not* to make you thirsty; it's to inspire you to think (and buy) Coke when you are. When you think of athletic shoes, Nike wants you to think of them. When you need tires, Goodyear wants you to remember their name. That's why they fly those blimps around…they just want you to remember their name and associate Goodyear with tires.

Our single most important strategy for reaching searchers for Christ is to be visible to them when they experience disruption. We'll come back and expand on that in a moment. But first, let's talk about the other kind of disruption.

Our most important strategy for reaching searchers for Christ is to be visible to them when they experience disruption.

POSITIVE DISRUPTION: OPPORTUNITY

There is another kind of disruption that I call *positive disruption*. When we see a better way, a role model, a tool that will make our work easier, or we read a book that inspires us toward improvement in something, that is positive disruption. We are inspired to make things better or to better ourselves. Our equilibrium has been shaken just like with negative disruption (we are no longer in even-keel or steady-state mode), but our response is a positive one: We want to improve. We go into growth mode. We aren't happy with our current state; we want a better one.

Positive disruption stimulates us by the comparison between what is and what can be. When we buy into the vision of a future that is better if only we owned a certain product, we'll buy that product. If life is good with 12 TV channels, think how much better it could be if we had 125. We aren't trying to get back to the middle; we're trying to move ahead.

We don't buy a vacation home to solve a problem; we buy because we visualize happy times with our families in carefree environments. Advertisers cast visions of us looking younger with Botox treatments, looking thinner after the Jenny Craig engagement, and looking cooler when we drive around in that new BMW convertible. All are opportunities for us to be the best; they just require us to part with our money for the products that will make us that way.

This is positive disruption. We buy into a vision. We seize an opportunity.

Positive disruption has a softer impact than negative disruption. We have to initiate, to imagine, to visualize before the idea can become a felt need. Negative disruption is a problem, and problems usually hurt. They have pain associated with them, so we're called to immediate action to solve problems. It's easier to put off buying into opportunities. What we have is getting us by, and there's always a little doubt whether it will really turn out as well for me as it has for the guy in the ads.

People who are beginning to search for God will be stimulated and driven by these same two motivators. They will have a problem that needs a solution, or they will grasp a vision of the person they could be. They might even experience both at the same time, as I did through my relationship with Charlie Childers.

DISRUPTION EVENTS: THE BEGINNING OF CHANGE

Charlie was one of my top account executives, and he had become ill. Charlie had contracted multiple myeloma, a horrible form of cancer that turns your bones into Swiss cheese.

As the leader of my organization, it was my job to visit Charlie and see to it that his job was getting done among the treatments and the hospital stays. Working for a large, well-respected company like AT&T, it was also my job to see that his needs were met and that his family was being taken care of.

But God had a plan that I wasn't aware of: to use my visits with Charlie to create disruption in my life and to move me into a search for His truth.

I had known Charlie for five or six years. He was a man's man—hunting, fishing, chewing tobacco, drinking with the guys and all of that. But Charlie started to change about a year before he became ill. When I would see him to review his accounts or go on sales calls, he was very different. Thoughtful, kind, mature, interested in me, not in impressing me as he had been before. There was something about Charlie that was different and compelling.

Until Charlie, I wanted to get as far away from sick people as I could. I suppose they scared me because they reminded me of my own mortality, and I wasn't in the mood to think about that. But I found myself calling Charlie to check on him and driving the one hundred miles each way to visit with him as his health declined. And I wasn't just doing my duty; I had become genuinely engaged with this kind, loving man who was getting sicker and sicker.

As the months dragged on and Charlie's condition worsened, I began to notice that he never wanted to talk about himself; he always wanted to talk about me. "How are you doing, Regi? How's Miriam? Tell me what's going on with Ross and Erin." There was a genuine interest in me, even though he was in ever-increasing pain.

The last time I saw Charlie alive, his condition was so horrible I can hardly describe it. The cancer had so weakened his spine that his head hung down and to the side. He struggled to breathe. He struggled to look up at me, even though I was kneeling beside his chair so that I could be at eye level with him.

He said, "Regi, don't feel sad for me. I know where I'm going. I just want you to think about what would happen to you if you were where I am."

On the long drive back home, I thought about what he said. What would happen to me? What do I really believe? How can he have such peace? How can he be focused on me while he is in so much pain and facing imminent death?

Charlie had credibility with me because he was a great salesperson. He also had credibility because he had gone public with his faith, and he did it *before* he became ill. And he had credibility with me because he continually expressed genuine interest in me.

Charlie started me on the path to finding peace. God used Charlie as the catalyst to move me from apathy to beginning to search…from an A to a B.

You see, Charlie wasn't a minister or a priest, he was an account executive. He was in the marketplace, and he was about his Father's business even to his death, reaching out to me, his boss, challenging me to reflect on the reality of my own mortality and on my need for peace in my life.

Charlie's illness was both a negative and a positive disruption for me. His was the first real encounter I had with someone my age who was dying. His last words to me—"What if this happened to you?"—were sobering. I hadn't considered the idea that I could get sick and die. I was too busy getting ahead.

And it was a positive disruption as well. I watched Charlie change after he committed to Christ. I heard the buzz about how his behavior both at the office and after hours had done a 180. He became a respected leader in his office. People loved him, even people who didn't care much for him before. I would hear "I'd do anything for that man" from his coworkers.

I wanted to be that kind of person. I wanted people to look up to me that way. I wanted to have the kind of peace and patience that I had seen in Charlie. God used Charlie to create positive disruption inside me. My search had begun in earnest. Charlie's death stirred something in me that was either new or had been lying dormant for years.

I have found that most strong Christians (the D's and E's on my grid) had some disruption in their lives that put them into "search mode." They had a problem and they began to search for a solution, or they saw a life that they admired and started trying to figure out what made that person different.

Most strong Christians had some disruption in their lives
that put them into "search mode."

Our search for God often starts when we first face an important situation and we have no control. We are helpless. It is out
of our hands, and we start to wonder if there is someone or
something out there whose hands it is in.

The closer the crisis is to us, the more intense our search will
be. Charlie's death started a search that was completed almost
two years later, and even then, it took a disruption of my own
for me to surrender to the Truth. Others that I know have
responded a lot faster, but the disruption was a lot more immediate.

So what are we to do with the B's on our grid?

I offer you three ideas for influencing B's: living out loud,
going on the journey with them, and consistent prayer.

LIVING OUT LOUD

"What you *are* thunders through so loudly, I can't hear what you
say to the contrary," said Ralph Waldo Emerson, a perennial
searcher.

Jesus' command in Matthew 6:33 is for us to "seek first his
kingdom and his righteousness." Jesus said it that way because
He knew that if we weren't seeking His kingdom, we wouldn't
put much emphasis on seeking His righteousness. But I believe
He wanted us to put those two things together, to see them as
interdependent. If we seek His kingdom without pursuing righ-

teousness, we won't make a whit of difference for His kingdom. We will have no moral authority. We won't be able to sell others on the food if we don't eat it ourselves.

People watch each other, keeping mental notes about how those in their lives can add value to theirs. When we need something, we will usually think, Who do I know that I can call on? When we need a cup of sugar, we think about the next-door neighbor. When we have a question about our dog's health, we think about our friend who is a vet. People are our most accessible, most economical, and most efficient source of information.

When a person gets interested in spiritual things, they're likely to look around at people they know and whom they think might have answers to their questions.

So, the most powerful thing that you can do to attract a searcher to Christ is to *be an authentic Christian and live like it.* Authenticity screams out in an inauthentic world. And people today have seen few examples of authentic Christianity. Mother Teresa certainly qualifies, but few can imagine themselves being that selfless. Billy Graham stands out as one who has been in the public eye for decades and has avoided the failures of so many other television preachers. Yet, who can visualize themselves as Billy Graham?

But God uses normal people to attract the attention of a searcher. These role models catch the searcher's eye with a different kind of life. It may be their loving smile and accepting attitude. It may be their family and their awesome kids. It may be the wisdom they display in sensitively managing the intricacies of business relationships. It may be all of the above, but there is something different about an authentic Christian life that is intriguing and attractive to the searcher.

So how do we live a life so compelling that a searcher will

be drawn to our authentic Christianity? I see three key dimensions to living out loud.

1. The allure of the absolute truth

À critical element to living out loud is a commitment to the absolute truth. Saying it another way, when we avoid dishonesty and don't compromise the truth, people notice. It is so rare in this era of spin and "every man for himself."

When we avoid dishonesty and don't compromise the truth, people notice.

We all recognize the active lie, the overt untruth. An *active* lie stretches the truth, embellishes the facts, reconstructs history, and sometimes just plain fabricates details to make the story work. These lies can be about important work-related issues, or they can be about after-work and weekend adventures, coworkers, or friends. But let a searcher catch a Christian in one of these lies, and it's curtains. "There, you see...just like everyone else I've ever known. Just making it up so they can make it through." Influence is nil. Game over.

Passive lying is similar, but actually offers an upside opportunity. Passive dishonesty is turning your head, letting it go when someone else is being dishonest or makes a mistake that benefits you. When the payroll department miscalculates your vacation days, and you have the chance to get an extra day off with pay if you just stay quiet, that's passive dishonesty. The opportunity comes when you call the payroll clerk and report the error. Why would someone be so honest? Not only will that person know of your honest act, but word spreads in an organization. One little thing, then another, then another...before long you are known as a person of stellar integrity, and you have additional influence.

They say that true character is demonstrated by what someone does when no one is looking. I believe that someone is almost always looking, and they will always be looking when, to your own hurt, you step forward and correct a mistake.

When Delta Air Lines first automated its frequent flyer program, they mistakenly added almost fifty thousand miles to my account. No one would have ever known.

Now I faced a dilemma. Do I call Delta and give up enough miles for a couple of free (but stolen) tickets, or do I keep the miles? I chose to call Delta. To my surprise, the agent said, "We don't have a procedure for taking miles out of an account. No one has ever called with a request like this before." I had a great conversation with the agent about how my honesty was between me and my Creator...not between me and Delta.

And those are the kinds of decisions that will enhance your influence in the workplace if you make them well, and will break your influence if you choose to compromise.

2. Giving away love

Beginning to Search B's are watching your life to see if you have something they admire and want. They are drawn to positive people who have positive ideas and attitudes. They are paying attention to what you say, but even more to what you do.

Loving others tops the list. When we are for people, regardless of their appearance, beliefs, behavior, or status, searchers are impressed. They are often "pro-people" themselves, and that can be one of the reasons they have an interest in spiritual things.

Tim Sanders, in his bestselling book *Love Is the Killer App*, says that we love people in the workplace by doing three things: sharing our knowledge, sharing our network, and showing compassion.

First, we share with people *knowledge* that will help them. If a fellow employee has an onerous mortgage but has no clue as to how to refinance for a lower rate, we can share our recent experience and help them understand how to refinance. Should they be considering leasing a car, we might pass along that pamphlet we picked up at the auto show that gives the pros and cons of leasing versus purchasing. If they are struggling with an issue and we have read a book about it, then we either loan them or give them the book. Whenever we have knowledge that will help them, we share it openly and generously.

Second, we offer our *network* of contacts to help them. If they need to paint their house, we tell them about the guy that did a great job painting our house. If they have a particular problem on the job, then we introduce them to every single person we know that might have ideas on how to solve it. We have nothing to gain; we help them because we have chosen to love them.

Finally, we show *compassion* for them. We show up when there's a crisis. We show them that we care when they don't get the promotion they so badly wanted. We reach out to them when they lose a loved one or suffer a family setback. We don't have to say much, we just have to show up.

Notice that all three of these are action oriented, not verbal. I've been taught that the only love that is real is love that is demonstrated. All three of Sander's love languages are about action over words, demonstration over verbalization. "They will know we are Christians by our love" is a true statement.

3. Avoiding the hot spots

Living out loud may mean staying quiet at times, even when we have so much we would like to say. Sometimes, the issues that come up are ones we hold deep-seated feelings about. We should have strong opinions and convictions if our lives are to line up with Scripture. So how do we stand firm for what we believe without turning off the searchers and others who are not Christians?

Most importantly, our *behavior* has to speak loudest about our convictions. Then if we are asked, we can talk about our positions calmly and with confidence. We can talk about things all day long, but it's what we do that resonates with people.

> We can talk about things all day long, but it's what we do that resonates with people.

We can talk about our disdain for pornography, but the magazines that we buy, the books we read, the movies we rent, and the websites we visit will say more about our true convictions than our words. And one trip to the gentlemen's club after work wipes out all the words we've said against porn.

Searching B's are looking for authenticity, and authenticity requires that our yes be yes and our no be no. So our first obligation as we attempt to live out loud is to make sure that our *walk completely matches our talk.*

Realistically, we are going to be faced with questions that are land mines. Where do you come out on homosexuality? Why do so many Christians oppose abortion and then use birth-control methods that create the same result? How can you support the commandment "You shall not murder" and then support the death penalty?

These can be genuine questions from thoughtful searchers, or they can be setups intended to get one more Bible thumper to bite the dust. How do we tell the difference and what do we do?

My experience is that it's best to avoid these questions for as long as you can, and make sure that you aren't the one who brings them up. I again point to Augustine: "In essentials, unity; in nonessentials, liberty; and in all things, charity." If we can keep searchers focused on the essentials (Jesus Christ, His deity, His death, and His resurrection), then we are less likely to get sidetracked.

If we can keep searchers focused on the essentials, then we are less likely to get sidetracked.

That's not to say that these other matters aren't important; they are. But they can wait until your coworker can examine them with a new heart through a Christian world view. Salvation is more important than sexuality, more important than any individual sin, and more important than any other doctrinal issue we can get into.

Once a searcher meets Christ, then Christ will lead that person toward His truth on all these contemporary issues.

GO ON THE JOURNEY WITH THEM

When Jesus said "Follow me" to His disciples, that was the beginning of a journey. Along the way, there were lessons they learned and lessons they failed to learn. Jesus recognized that they weren't going to get it all at once. We should recognize that as well.

Unfortunately, many Christian evangelists can't wait to get folks to pray the prayer, so they rush people past their sincere questions and hang-ups just so they can get them to say the magic words, expressing their belief in Jesus. Scripture is pretty clear that there are no magic words anyway; it's the heart that has to speak its faith.

When a column B person is sincerely searching for Truth, go on the search with them. When someone says, "I really can't buy into this idea that there's only one way to God," we are so tempted to lower the boom with John 14:6 ("I am the way and the truth and the life. No one comes to the Father except through me"). "Hey, Jesus said it, not me. There it is, in black and white. You just need to know the truth, because the truth will set you free." Conversation over.

Far better that we learn to respond this way: "You know, that is a tough one. I've struggled with that one myself. What are some other ways to God? Which of those are you seriously considering? Let's look into what those approaches have to offer and compare them to Christianity."

Then, if you have to read a book about a new age religion or a cult that the person is considering, you'll be equipped to show your friend where the alternatives all break down when compared to Christ.

My friend Craig came hustling into our breakfast place one morning with a huge smile on his face. "I think I've found it. This book is incredible!" he said as he plopped down a copy of *The Celestine Prophecy* by James Redfield.

"Wow, I don't think I've ever heard you say that before," I replied. "Must be a profound book."

As he talked about the insights in the book, it was all I could do to restrain myself. I wanted to scream, "New age junk! Beware! Danger!" But I resisted the temptation. Instead, I said, "Hey, how about if I read it and then let's talk about it?"

"That would be awesome," Craig replied, truly excited that I would take an interest in this new "truth" he had found.

I read the book and made notes about the things that I found that were in conflict with Scripture (and there were plenty). I also noted that there were nine insights. None of them told me how to live or raise my kids.

So when Craig and I got back together several weeks later, he couldn't wait to hear what I thought about his new book of truth. I showed him the points that I had grave disagreement with, and contrasted the book with the truth in the Bible. It may have been the first time in a long time that Craig had touched a Bible, as he sat there reading the Scriptures that I had highlighted.

"You know, I wonder if there will be another insight?" I mused. "When this book's sales start to slump, and the author has had some more time to write, I bet there'll be a tenth insight. Wouldn't it be awful to build your life around someone's nine philosophical ideas only to have them come out with a tenth sometime later on?" I asked.

Sure enough, about a year later, Warner Books published a new treatise by Redfield called *The Tenth Insight*.

Now Craig didn't become a Christian because I read a new age book that he was hot on. But my influence with Craig was strengthened because I was willing to go with him on his search; I didn't try to shortcut the journey or try to convince him to omit steps that he wanted to take along the way.

This patience and persistence is possible when we remember that it is not our job to save someone. God determines outcomes. We are to help those in our sphere of influence to take next steps, even when the next steps are not heading in a straight line for the kingdom.

As you travel with them on their journey, remember that Beginning to Search B's aren't repelled by one's genuine love for God. They are curious about it, even drawn to it when it's authentic.

When you pause to pray silently over your food at lunchtime, people notice. When people know that you're very involved in your church, they pay attention. When you avoid the gossip circles, hang out with the positive employees, and do great work on your job, people remember.

When you handle disappointment with grace, it stands out. When you don't laugh at the crude joke, it's silently noted. When you include everyone in your conversations, you're making a statement that gets heard.

We don't have to numb down our faith to make it attractive. Just the opposite is true. The more Christian we are in our words and particularly in our deeds, the more attractive our faith is to others.

Searchers' journeys get more challenging as they begin to zero in on Truth. They need information that moves their general belief in God to specific belief in Jesus Christ. I mentioned earlier Lee Strobel's book *The Case for Christ*. It is an excellent book that leads the reader from general faith to specific faith. There are several other books that have a similar motive, including *How Good Is Good Enough* by Andy Stanley.

Your personal story is often the most powerful resource that you can offer. As you describe your doubts, your meanderings, and your own path to discovering Truth, your searcher friend can relate because he knows you. And if your walk matches up with your talk, your story will have a strong impact on his search. And as to authenticity, I go back to my favorite story from the Gospels, the man blind from birth. This man said (paraphrased), "Hey, I don't know the answers to all your questions. I just know that I was blind, and now I can see."

Over the years, the church has lost the freshness and clarity of this story. This man was just telling people what had happened to him. He didn't need any training, any tracts, or any techniques. He simply needed the courage to tell people what he had experienced, what he was a *witness* to!

Peel and Larimore point this out to be one of the biggest corruptions of what Jesus intended for us to do. We were instructed to *be* "witnesses"—that is, people who experienced something ourselves and then reported it. Over the years, well-meaning active Christians turned that into "witnessing," a verb, something we're supposed to *do*.

Write out your story. Get comfortable with telling it, in both long and short versions. Be as transparent as you can bring yourself to be. And when the time is right, tell your story. If you can't tell it, hand over a copy of what you wrote. People can argue with you all day long about the Bible, but no one can argue with your personal experience.

No one can argue with your personal experience.

As you create your IMAP and become intentional in your work relationships, you will find yourself accumulating sermons, articles, and books that you know you can use to help your coworkers take their next steps. There's no better set of resources than those that you have already "consumed" and that you can share with the strength of your own convictions and experience. Our church gives away a free CD that includes a talk called "Intimacy with God." That presentation gives searchers the basic biblical information they need to understand the gospel. (You can go to http://resources.northpoint.org/store to purchase this CD. In addition, there is a great tool there that allows you to search for a subject or issue, and the website will point you to a relevant CD. It's pretty cool!)

CONSISTENT PRAYER

B's are just one step away from salvation. I can get fired up to pray when the big step is just one step away. For me, it's easier to pray for something when it looks achievable. When I see someone who has a basic belief in God, who is actively seeking truth and just needs to accept the truth of Jesus as the Son of God and their Savior, I can pray with a lot more faith. I know that may not be biblical, but it's a true confession.

When I interact with the B's on my list, I am building the relationship toward the day when I can ask, "What are the three biggest questions or hang-ups that keep you from accepting Jesus Christ for who He says He is?" Once someone shares that information, I *really* know how to pray for him or her. I can ask God to put someone in that person's life to answer question number 1. I can ask God to point me to a Scripture, a book, or a sermon that will help him find the answer to question number 2. I can ask God to directly intervene and give him the answer to question number 3. Each day, I can pray that God will use whatever means necessary to get that person's questions answered.

And when I talk to that B the next time, I can ask about one of those questions. Remember, he is searching, looking for answers with you and on his own. You are on the journey with him, so you aren't prying when you ask about his search. You're just checking in, the same as you might if he were preparing to sit for his CPA exam.

> You are on the journey with him, so you aren't prying when you ask about his search.

Praying for B's can be invigorating because they are so close to the biggest decision of their lives, but I still recommend that you pray for all the people on your IMAP grid. Ask God, "Who on this grid do you want me to pray for today?" and then obey. Then ask God, "Who on this grid do you want me to touch today...and how?" Over and over, He has shown me the names to pray for, and over and over, He has led me to call, write, e-mail, or visit with just the right person at just the right time.

CLOSING THE DEAL: FROM SEARCHING (B)
TO CONFESSING (C)

It's been said that a person coming to faith in Christ is a process. It's like a chain, with links all connected to each other. One event leads to another event, which leads to another. Link by link, the chain finally leads to that final link when the person crosses over that line of faith and believes. No link in the chain can be left out; no one link is more or less important than another. You may or may not get to be there when God draws your friend or colleague into a personal relationship with Himself. I often ask God to let me be there, and on a few occasions, He has blessed me with that opportunity.

But that is not critical. What really matters is that it happens—that B's become C's; that searchers go from a macro belief in God to a micro belief in the Son of God, Jesus Christ, as their Lord and Savior.

We talked about the four key words that Jesus used in John 3:16—God *loved*, God *gave*, I *believe*, and I *receive*. That is as simple as it gets, and if you ever have the opportunity to be there when a B decides to trust Christ, you can fall back on that simple, four-word road map to get through a prayer that will express their newfound faith in Christ. I know that scares you to death, but you can do it. Besides, these aren't magic words that have to be said a certain way; it's about the person's heart and the sincerity of their surrender to the Truth.

When my next-door neighbor called one day to tell me he was "ready to have peace" in his life, I called our pastor. When he got to Ken's office, Ken had his whole family there. Both Ken and his daughter received Christ that day, and his wife and son reaffirmed their commitment to the Lord. What pastor wouldn't be delighted to make that house call?

In chapter 9, we will talk about developing relationships with other Christians in your workplace, of teaming up with others who are about our Father's business at work. As you learn your teammates' gifts and talents, you may find that God has put someone in your sphere of influence who is just the perfect person to close the deal with a B who has successfully completed his search.

There is also the possibility that a B will want to settle things with God all by himself. Over the last two years, two of my B's have gone into an empty bedroom, gotten down on their knees, and asked Christ to come into their hearts. Our face-to-face involvement is sometimes helpful, even necessary...but not always.

REALISM, NOT FATALISM

When Jesus looked at Peter and asked pointedly, "Who do *you* say that I am?" He asked the one question that everyone has to confront. It's the question that determines our eternal destination. B's ultimately have to face that question, and although I don't know why it's this way, some are going to get it and some aren't. If we have loved and accepted our B's in an unconditional way, if we have lived a godly life out loud in front of them, if we have gone on the journey with them, helping them pursue the answers to their questions, and if we have prayed earnestly for our searcher friends to come to Christ, we have done our jobs and done them well. The outcome is up to God. Remember, "No one can come to me," Jesus said, "unless the Father who sent me draws him" (John 6:44).

Some are going to get it and some aren't.

Stop for a moment right now and pray for those you know who are B's. Ask God to point you to the Beginning to Search person that He wants you to "touch" next. Ask Him to give you both wisdom and courage as you attempt to guide these searching souls' next steps toward the Savior.

CALLING THE CHOSEN FROZEN

I CALL THE PEOPLE IN COLUMN C *CONFESSING* OR *CHRISTIAN*. These people will say they believe that Jesus Christ is God's Son. They may attend church or be an inactive member. Some C's have vast knowledge of the Bible and church history, and may have led Sunday school or Bible studies. C's can often be sincere in their faith, but are more comfortable keeping personal things personal.

The factor that distinguishes Confessing C's from other Christians is that their lives lack outward evidence of growth. C's may still be harboring sinful behaviors and not exhibit any of the fruit of the Spirit. In everyday situations, they will make little or no reference to their faith. They are just what the word says...passive!

Now I must remind us that only God knows what's really going on in someone's heart. We are not to judge. And that's the furthest thing from my intention here. It's just that God has called us to be good stewards of the relationships around us, and that begins by trying to understand as much as we can about the spiritual climate inside. Paul wrote, "I have become all things to all men so that by all possible means I might save some" (1 Corinthians 9:22). In order to be anything to anyone, we must first pay attention to where they are in their journey toward God.

C IS FOR COMPLICATED

When it comes to being about my Father's business, Confessing C's have often been the most perplexing category for me. Put me with an Apathetic A and I get excited. Show me a Beginning to Search B and I'll lie awake at night thinking of ways to help them take the next step. But put me with a C and I can start to feel rigor mortis setting in.

> Confessing C's have often been the most perplexing category for me.

At least when I'm with a Developing D or an Excelling E, I can learn something. But there's something about being around C's that makes me feel about as useful as a blind man's flashlight.

Hang with me for a minute here. I'm not saying they're not important. I'm just being honest that it has taken me years to fully understand how to motivate this group to take the next step. C's can be really frustrating if you don't see the diamond in the coal. There have been times, as far as I was concerned, when C could have stood for counterfeit, caricature, or crock. I mean, how could someone have an authentic relationship with Christ, the Lord of the universe, and not appear the least bit energized by it?

Jesus warned about the dangers of being lukewarm and of salt losing its flavor. But before we too impulsively spew this group out of our mouths, let me suggest that sometimes a C is really a D in need of a push. That's the key with all these categories. You have to picture each one of them taking the next step...one step at a time.

PUT ON YOUR SPURS

There's something inside all of us that resists the idea of telling people how they should live their lives. *Faith is a personal matter that deserves our respect, so who am I to critique someone else's interpretation of Christianity?* And when it comes to the C's, you may feel especially uncomfortable trying to influence their faith. *They already claim to believe in Jesus, so why am I rocking their boat? Why should I risk offending them?*

But you must feel the same sense of mission with C's that you feel for those who are unbelievers. If indeed the people you identify as C's are believers, then you may actually have a greater responsibility to them than you have to people in the other categories. The Bible contains more instructions on how believers should live with other believers than on how to share our faith with unbelievers. The writer of Hebrews, for example, commands us to "spur one another on toward love and good deeds" (Hebrews 10:24). Jesus commanded us to make disciples, not just believers.

> You must feel the same sense of mission with C's that you feel for those who are unbelievers.

Why does the Bible talk so much about how we should act toward other Christians? Because God knows that a community of believers in relationship with each other will always be a better evangelism tool than one lone-ranger Christian. Even if you don't see eye to eye on everything, the fact that you agree on the major themes (such as salvation by grace and the deity of Christ) can be very noteworthy to the unbeliever. In fact, your diversity may make Christ even more attractive because the unbeliever is less likely to think that Christianity requires him to look or act a certain way.

In addition, fellow believers have the most potential to become disciplemakers themselves. After all, they already believe. And if they go on to become Excelling E's, it could end up being the most productive use of your time and energy. Perhaps no one has ever challenged these C's to be more bold and intentional with their faith. Maybe God has put you into their lives to encourage them toward a more exciting relationship with their Lord.

WILL THE REAL C'S PLEASE STAND UP?

Now before you assume that your C is truly a believer, I want to offer one more observation: many Confessing C's are actually Apathetic A's in disguise. In our culture, it's easy for people to lump themselves in with the cultural Christians. *Of course I'm a Christian. I'm an American, aren't I?*

Many Confessing C's are actually Apathetic A's in disguise.

When I first met Kenny, it didn't take me long to conclude that he was a C. During one of our earliest conversations, I shared an experience that had happened at a men's retreat years before. At the mere mention of a church function, Kenny opened up about his experience growing up in the church. Our conversation lasted about ten minutes, and in that time I'd heard enough from Kenny to convince me that he was a believer in Jesus Christ.

But as I got to know Kenny better in the weeks and months that followed, some things just didn't add up. It was clear that he had many beliefs that simply weren't consistent with faith in Christ. For example, he believed that all people are a part of God—not just connected to God in relationship, but actually pieces of God. He also thought that salvation came as a result of being in touch with your connection to God. As it turned out, Kenny was quite pantheistic or new age in his beliefs. And when it came to Jesus Christ, Kenny had very little desire to draw near to Him or learn more about Him.

Upon these discoveries, I quickly moved Kenny from the C column over to the A column. Even though he had grown up attending a mainline Christian church and professed to be aligned with Christianity, Kenny was actually a full-blown apathetic.

Since then, I have observed that there are many apathetics who grew up in church-attending homes and therefore know a lot about Christianity. But when it comes to their core beliefs, there's not much that resembles faith in Christ. In fact, sometimes A's will use their knowledge of Christianity to avoid being bothered by born-again Christians. They've learned that if they just talk the talk, the Christians will soon move on to someone else.

This is an important distinction to make. Imagine if I had continued to pursue Kenny as if he were a C. Instead, I was able to love and accept Kenny where he was. I moved alongside him as a caring friend, waiting and praying for God to bring a disruption in his life that might cause him to search for better answers.

So before you label someone a C, you'll want to be sure you've really gotten to know him on the inside. Only then can you serve his true need.

JUST ADD COURAGE

One of the prominent verbs used throughout the New Testament is the word *encourage*. Of all the words used to describe how believers should treat each other, encouragement stands out as the ultimate. Implicitly, someone who encourages is already deeply engaged in an exuberant pursuit of Christ. In addition, authentic encouragement is a selfless act. It bears overtones of humility and a willingness to invest in someone else at great personal expense.

Interestingly, *encourage* can be broken down into two parts: "en" (or "in") and "courage." The word means "to put courage in." That's a great word picture for what it means to encourage your C's to take the next step. Through your friendship and support, you can actually give them the courage they need to move out of their comfort zones. It's amazing how much more appealing the Christian life is when you have someone else to walk through it with you—someone to bear the burdens and share the celebrations.

Conversely, being an outspoken Christian is politically incorrect today. It's easy to feel alone and isolated. So it's no wonder C's often have a long list of reasons for keeping a low profile and a very short list of reasons to make waves, especially at work. But when you take a look around, you may discover a surprising number of C's who are receptive to some motivation and encouragement. When you invite them to pursue a deeper relationship with Christ, it might be just what they've been looking for in their quest for purpose in life. Spiritual growth is always exponential when it's attached to a cause. Your unspoken challenge to honor Christ in the workplace could be the cause that ignites a new season of growth in their lives.

> C's often have a long list of reasons for keeping a low profile and a very short list of reasons to make waves.

A CAUSE WORTH LIVING FOR

That's the universal trigger point for C's—a cause. It's the key to waking them up from spiritual hibernation. The typical C has spent much of his life in and around the church. But oftentimes, his level of Christian activity far exceeds his level of true spiritual activity. As seminary professor Howard Hendricks describes it, Christians everywhere have been immunized against a meaningful relationship with Christ. Their souls have been exposed to a dead version of Christianity for so long that the real thing never gets a chance.

What's missing is a reason for doing things differently. Of course, that reason can always be introduced through a negative disruption that forces a test of the person's faith. But when it comes to C's, the discovery of a new cause can be very effective as a positive disruption. There's something about a cause that moves ideas from a person's head down to his heart.

A cause is a short-term objective that is the personification of a long-term personal value.

The Promise Keepers movement is a great example of how a cause can stir someone to examine and express their beliefs. In the 1990s, men from across the country began filling football stadiums for the purpose of presenting themselves to God. As the event was repeated, word traveled. Soon, tens of thousands of men were attending each year, and Promise Keepers' status was elevated from event to phenomenon. In that transition, a cause was born. Suddenly, Promise Keepers was more than just an opportunity to express devotion to God. It was tantamount to a referendum. The trip to the stadium became a pilgrimage, a time for Christian men to stand up and be counted. At its peak, Promise Keepers was drawing hundreds of thousands of C's to an event they otherwise would have ignored. Not because the movement appealed to their style of Christianity, but because they were intrigued by the cause it cultivated. And in the process of attending, many of those C's were swept into a new season of spiritual growth.

On a smaller scale, your interaction with the C's in your office can have a similar effect. Sometimes all a C needs is an invitation to begin seeking God's presence in a new environment, in a new way.

That was the case for my friend Paul. Paul was a growing, passionate Christian who had a heart for several men in his office who were C's. Five years earlier, Paul had been a C himself. And now that he was enjoying his newfound intimacy with Christ, he longed for his friends to experience it, too.

Paul prayed that God would draw the men to Himself. He had no problem accepting them because he related to them so well. As a result, Paul felt very comfortable inviting them to form a small men's group for a period of eight weeks. He began by approaching Dan, the most outspoken of the other believers in the company, and presenting the idea of reading a Christian book together. They would read one chapter per week from *The Man in the Mirror*, a book on men's issues, and then meet over lunch in the conference room each Wednesday to discuss their opinions. Paul also shared the names of four other men he wanted to include.

One by one Paul presented his idea to the other men. He would say, "I've always thought it would be interesting to bond a little with the other Christians in our office. It's not meant to be a burdensome commitment; we can just give it a try for a few weeks and see what happens."

Knowing that four other men were considering the idea proved persuasive. Paul's efforts put courage in the men to examine their beliefs together. He appealed to the Christian convictions that already existed in each man and provided a cause to hang them on. Their numbers, though relatively small, provided a sense of security. And eventually, all five agreed to join Paul's group.

The concept of a Christian meeting that wasn't affiliated with a church was new to most of them. They had never considered the need to pursue God apart from Sunday morning. And the suggestion that God is not confined to the four walls of the church building was an important revelation. Furthermore, being part of a new venture made being a Christian an exciting part of each man's identity. It broadened their spiritual horizons and made them feel like part of something bigger than the church-sized God they had grown accustomed to. When a C is pushed beyond his boundaries, it can lead to many exciting discoveries.

The group meetings proved to be rich and rewarding. For the first time in their lives, three of the men were exposed to the concept of developing a personal relationship with Christ (the topic of our next chapter on Developing D's). One of the men stuck with it and matured quickly as a believer. And although it didn't blossom right away with the others, at least the seed was planted.

The Confessing Christian needs challenges. An important part of gaining influence with these believers is to express interest in their personal faith. Instead of feeling threatened, they begin to feel valued and affirmed. Rather than offend by implying that they aren't real Christians, ask if they'd be willing to have lunch and talk about what it's like to be a Catholic or a Methodist or whatever their "brand" is. Ask them for permission to challenge them. Ask them if they'd be willing to challenge you. Call them your fellow believer and invite them into a friendship in which you encourage each other to experience God more significantly.

When you invite a C to connect with you as a fellow

believer, it neutralizes many of the obstacles that would otherwise exist. Obviously, you must authentically accept the person in order to develop this camaraderie. It's not about trying to enlighten him to your superior version of Christianity. It's inviting him to join together with you in a mutually encouraging relationship.

One of the best things about C's is that they often have a long history of Bible exposure. Though the books may be dusty, the library is full. And once the flames are fanned a little, they are often equipped for rapid growth and expeditious maturity because of the head knowledge they possess. It's just a matter of rebooting the old system.

C's often have a long history of Bible exposure. Though the books may be dusty, the library is full.

Deep down, each of us desires to be included in something significant. Confessing C's are no exception. They need to see Christianity—their Christianity—portrayed in a new way. If you can help them see that their faith has relevance in everyday life, they can begin to experience a relationship with God that's more vibrant than they ever thought possible. Keep in mind that most Confessing C's have God confined to a small segment of their lives and have never been shown the relevance of their faith to their work. In fact, author Doug Sherman estimates that over 90% percent of all church attenders have never heard a sermon that relates the Bible to the workplace.[5]

One of the greatest things about the Billy Graham

Evangelistic Association is how it stirs new activity in the local church. Whenever Billy Graham plans a crusade, his organization reaches out to the churches in the area. This affirms the local churches, and at the same time creates a positive disruption to fan the flames throughout each congregation. As they are invited to participate in the crusade, they are confronted with the idea of putting action behind their beliefs. It causes them to contemplate the meaning behind some of the old traditions. It invites them to ponder relevant ways to express a faith that sometimes goes back several generations.

That's what it looks like to be about your Father's business in the life of a Confessing C. Challenge them, involve them in a cause, spur them on to good works, but do so with a gentle touch. Your heavenly Father prods you with plenty of sensitivity and encouragement. And that's how we are to treat these fellow believers.

DEVELOPING DISCIPLES

From Passive to Active

PART OF THE FUN OF BEING ABOUT YOUR FATHER'S BUSINESS each day is finding another disciple in your sphere of influence. You're trucking along, going about your work when somehow you discover that someone you know—one of the owners of the company, one of the sales reps that calls on you, one of the vendors that serves your company—is a dedicated follower of Christ.

It's like you've found a long-lost cousin who grew up in your hometown and who's familiar with all of the things that made home special. You can't wait to talk to him, get to know him, hear his story, start sharing life with him.

Developing D's are disciples—learners and followers of Christ. They aren't silent or secretive about their faith. Hang around them a little while and you'll pick up on the fact that they are believers.

D's on my IMAP grid are *doing something* to learn and grow. That's what distinguishes them from the chosen frozen. They participate in some intentional, structured activity—something more than attending worship on Sunday morning—for the purpose of pursuing God.

Learners are sponges; they soak up and internalize information. It's not just "how much can I know," it's also "how can I use this to help myself and others." D's read; they join small groups and Bible study classes; they listen to sermons; they even go to conferences and seminars. I distinguish a D from a C by their involvement in some regular, identifiable activity that has growth in their Christian faith as its objective.

Followers are soldiers; they ask for instructions and they follow the orders their Commanding Officer gives them. God gives all disciples certain instructions through His Word. True followers follow those instructions, universal orders such as "Love your neighbor as yourself," "Honor your father and your mother," and "Do not commit adultery." We all have these instructions in common. They are universal for all of His followers.

But God also gives specific, individual instructions to His developing disciples. The difference might just be that D's are tuned in enough to hear them and committed enough to follow them. "Call Pete" comes clearly into my head as I pray over my IMAP. "Stop and help that lady" says the little voice as I see the traffic begin to bog down behind the car stalled in the intersection. These are the individual orders that God gives His disciples, orders that build His kingdom and our faith as we follow them.

THE DIFFERENCE BETWEEN IT AND HIM

In the last chapter, we talked about Confessing C's—people who say they believe in Jesus Christ but show little of the fruit of a relationship with God. C's often refer to Christianity as *it*, a set of beliefs, the most important of which is that Jesus Christ was God's Son and that He died on a cross to pay for their sins. If we perceive faith in Christ as a box to be checked off, then we're probably a C. We confess Christ; we're Christians; we're going to heaven. Case closed. Since we have it, we can go about life as usual.

But D's sense that there is something more…a lot more. D's know that confessing Jesus Christ is the beginning of a relationship, not the end of a quest for truth. D's refer to *Him* rather than *it*. Their relationship is personal. God is real to them. *Christian* is something they are, not something they assent to.

D's know that confessing Jesus Christ is the beginning of a relationship, not the end of a quest for truth.

Developing D's know that Christ came "that they may have life, and have it to the full" (John 10:10). They don't see their faith as something confined to the building with stained glass windows called church. They know a personal God who loves them and is available to them 24-7.

A Developing D is learning to pray constantly about everything and to recognize God's voice when He answers. A disciple is committed to the Bible. He recognizes it as God's message to us all and that it holds accurate answers to the significant questions that ultimately matter. D's are learning to connect the truths, stories, and illustrations from the Bible to their everyday lives. They are distilling principles to live their lives by, to guide their decisions, and to help them understand the events and circumstances of life through the lens of a Christian worldview. They are learning to see people as God sees them and to interpret and respond to events by realizing that God is in control and that nothing that happens escapes His attention. They are learning that He is always there, walking through the hills and the valleys right beside them...coaching them, encouraging them, challenging them, and always loving them.

D's are grateful people. They acknowledge the hand of God in their lives, turning their lives into something worth living and adopting them into His family. They give God the credit for their successes and for the blessings they've been given. Their lives are marked by gratitude and humility.

D's are on a journey, following the Master and learning from Him every day. And the journey won't end. They will never know it all or get it all down, at least not in this life. But they have joyfully committed to the trip, and they're delighted when they find a fellow traveler among their workmates.

THREE DIRECTIONS FOR GROWTH

A few years ago, our family was drawn to a new church in our city. That church, through several twists and turns, became North Point Community Church, now one of the fastest growing churches in the nation.

North Point promotes the idea that disciples of Jesus Christ need to be concerned with three vital relationships: intimacy with God, fellowship with insiders, and influence with outsiders. As I look back over these twenty-plus years that I've been about my Father's business, this trilogy helps me to organize and communicate what God has taught me about dealing with developing disciples in the workplace. The three vital relationships represent three directions for us to grow in, three disciplines to focus on, all at the same time.

1. Intimacy with God

Nothing is more important than this vital relationship, and there are two primary connections that God has given us for intimacy with Him.

Nothing is more important than intimacy with Him.

The first connection is the *Bible*. I can't explain how it came to be (there are books on apologetics that do that), but I can tell you it is a supernatural book. I know it from my own experience. Somehow, God put into this book a complete picture of Himself, and when we read and study it from that perspective, the Bible comes alive. When we ask, "Lord, what are You telling me about Yourself here?" God will start to communicate with us through His Word, giving us His perspective on the events and circumstances we face.

When we read in the Gospels the words of Jesus as He was confronted with different challenges, we learn to relax because we know that the Father who loved and cared for Him also loves and cares for us.

A friend told me about a dad who was diagnosed with terminal cancer. The dad, who had three small children, wrote a long letter to his kids telling them all about his life, including his successes and failures and how he had responded to them. He shared some of the principles that he had learned to be true, and through the stories of his own life, he showed his kids how those principles had helped him. He gave his kids a few stern dos and don'ts, based on his greater and often painful experiences. But in general, the letter was a hopeful expression of his love for his kids and a guide to help them fulfill a bright and promising future. He ended the letter with a description of what it would be like when this life had played out for each of them and they were in heaven together, a family reunited. The effect of that letter on those kids was profound.

If we had a letter like that from our dad, would we read it, study it, memorize it? We would read it over and over to work its truth down into our souls. We would look for every opportunity to be like that great dad…to do all the things he told us to do and to avoid every danger that he warned us about. We would make copies of that letter and carry it with us wherever we went. When we were a little down, we'd pull out that letter and remind ourselves of how much our dad loved us…how special we were to him, and how someday out there in the future, we were going to see and talk to him again.

The Bible is our letter. God is our perfect Father.

The second connection is through *prayer*. Just like with any relationship, intimacy grows in direct proportion to the amount and quality of the time that we spend with another person. If we spend unhurried time with God, if we listen as much as we talk, we can begin to relax in our relationship with Him and really get to know Him. When we learn to "be still and know that He is God," we can begin to pray without a checklist of things we want Him to do for us or people that we want Him to touch. We can begin to pray for who He wants us to pray for, and we can begin to experience intimacy with our heavenly Father and our best friend.

Intimacy grows in direct proportion to the amount and quality of the time that we spend with another person.

So much of intimacy depends on the mind-set and the attitude of our hearts when we approach God. Take a quick check of your status. Here are a few questions to ask:

- Is my heart soft toward God right now?
- Am I feeling empathetic or judgmental toward others right now?
- When I think of my wife or husband, does my heart smile or frown?
- If I am frowning, am I willing to forgive, right now, whatever it is that I am holding against them?
- Have I thought about or prayed for anyone today who is in trouble?
- Have I sincerely thanked God today for anything?

If the answer to any of these questions brought a sigh to your spirit, stop right now and talk to God. Tell Him how you answered the question. Ask Him to change your attitude—to help you forgive, to direct your thoughts to the friend who is in trouble right now. Thank Him for loving you, for adopting you into His family, for being so generous toward you.

You see, that's what intimacy is. It's constantly taking a check on your heart and constantly interacting with your heavenly Father to stay in step with Him. We are so ready to charge off telling everyone else how to be disciples, yet we miss out on the joy of having this intimate, minute-by-minute interaction with a kind, loving, understanding God.

Intimacy with God means bringing Him into every situation we face. When it comes to relationships, it's me, you, and God. "How would You have me react, Father? Give me the words that You would have me say." In every circumstance, it's, "What are You teaching me here, Father?"—then listening to and remembering what comes into your mind and heart. Intimacy is telling God when you're afraid, telling Him when you're tired, telling Him when you're disappointed...even angry. God knows what's in our hearts. He's big enough and loves us enough that He isn't going to be put off by us telling Him the truth about how we feel at a given moment.

And how are we to promote intimacy with God at work? By being intimate with God ourselves. When we develop and maintain an intimate relationship with our heavenly Father, we will be constantly filled with the Spirit of God. And when that happens, we are filled with love, joy, peace, patience, kindness, goodness, faithfulness, gentleness, and self-control. A person who consistently exhibits these qualities will stick out like black socks with Bermuda shorts. People will notice. People will ask, "How do you maintain such a wonderful attitude, day in and day out?"

And then you'll have the opportunity to tell them what you

do every day. It won't be hard to do, since you aren't preaching a sermon. You're just describing the way that you interact with a Very Important Person in your life, day by day.

2. *Fellowship with insiders*

It can be pretty lonely out there. But Developing D's seem to always find each other at work. Almost like alumni of the same university, they connect somehow. There is the common bond of love for God. There is the Spirit of God within these people that leads them to find one another.

When we have fellowship with insiders (i.e., those who are already in Christ), we have love in our lives. God loves us through other believers, His other children, our spiritual brothers and sisters.

Because we share the same priorities and values, we find it easier to show our love for other Christians. They accept and admire us; they don't look down on us or think we're crazy, because if we are, they are!

There is accountability in our relationships with insiders at work. One of my sayings is, "We all do better when somebody's looking." When our workmates know what we stand for, we know that they're watching how we act, how we conduct ourselves under pressure, how we behave when no one is looking. We'll think twice before we say things, lose our temper, or join in on things we shouldn't.

We have a lot to look forward to at the office when we work with other believers.

"What's God been doing in your life?" "What has He been teaching you?" "How can I pray for you this week?" It's just cool to share the work journey with others who are about my Father's business.

It's cool to share the work journey with others who are about my Father's business.

I'm often asked, "Shouldn't I look for a job in a Christian company, like yours?" I raise eyebrows when I declare that there is no such thing as a Christian company. Companies are legal entities created to limit the liability of their owners. Companies don't have souls and can't go to heaven, although I've heard of a bunch that sound like a living hell here on earth.

But I do believe that we can create Christian-friendly companies. Companies such as Chick-fil-A and ServiceMaster have long histories of creating environments where employees are encouraged to connect with and serve God.

As the leader in my business, I have led in creating events and environments that made it easy for the Christians in the company to find each other. Sponsoring a community service project facilitated by a Christian ministry will bring believers together, if not to do the physical work, then to help raise money or coordinate the effort. At our second company, InterServ, we built a Habitat-type house in the inner city through a Christian ministry called Charis. Some of us swung hammers on Saturdays, some washed cars and baked cakes, and some planned and coordinated the schedule of volunteers. It was a "win" to do good for people less fortunate, and also a "win" as the Christians in the company began to find each other and connect.

Many committed Christian business owners have almost created churches in their companies. They have corporate chaplains, worship services and Bible studies, prayer groups, and all sorts of ministry involvements from helping and serving the poor to Christian day care for employees' children.

While I certainly can't criticize any of these activities, my experience says that we're better served to encourage employees to get involved in a good church rather than try to create one in our business. An active, Christ-centered church is equipped to minister to the whole family, not just the employee. Great churches are focused; they are about meeting the needs of disciples and their families. That's what they do. Businesses and organizations have earthly duties to fulfill, even though the people who work there are (I hope) about their Father's business as they fulfill those duties. Sometimes, by trying to do two very different things at the same time, we can end up lackluster in both.

So D's are hooking up with other Christians, giving and receiving love, giving and receiving accountability, praying for and being prayed for. Through their relationships with other Christians at work, they have a work family...they belong. And as they go forward, they will be on the lookout for new employees who are insiders, people they can embrace and help to get connected with their brothers and sisters at work.

3. Influence with outsiders

I'm not particularly fond of the term *outsiders*, but I didn't come up with it. Paul did. Three different times (Colossians 4:5, 1 Thessalonians 4:12, and 1 Timothy 3:7), Paul refers to those outside the church. On our IMAP grid, these are the Apathetic A's and the Beginning to Search B's.

As we said before, Developing D's are committed, growing followers of Jesus Christ. They have love, joy, peace, patience, kindness, goodness, faithfulness, gentleness, and self-control.

Those qualities will make them stand out in any crowd. And with that attention comes responsibility, and with responsibility comes opportunity.

The only thing that differentiates a D from an E is that Excelling E's are intentional in their efforts to infect others with their faith in Christ. D's want Christ in their lives, but they are still focused on what He can do for them. Their faith is more self-centered. E's have gone beyond that; they want Him for themselves, but they also want others to know Him.

> D's want Christ in their lives, but they are still focused on what He can do for them.

Don't take this as an indictment of committed disciples of Jesus Christ. As I have said repeatedly, our spiritual journey consists of a series of steps. We move forward one step at a time. Sometimes several steps are taken in rapid succession, but it's often years between steps. For the person who becomes a Christian, the three steps are clear: from Confessing to Developing to Excelling....from column C to column D to column E!

C's have got it. D's are growing it. E's are giving it away.

And by the way, I'm glad there is sometimes a season between someone becoming a Christian and starting to share his faith. I could have saved a lot of pain in my family relationships had I taken some time to grow it before I started trying to give it away.

When I committed myself totally to Jesus Christ in 1983, I wanted everyone in my family to get right with God. I started handing out spiritual advice left and right. I called my brother, my sister, my mom, my dad…I was challenging everyone to give everything over to Jesus.

If someone had coached me to use a little restraint, I would have been a lot better off. Dr. Ross Campbell, a noted psychologist, says that unsolicited advice given to an adult is almost always received as criticism. I've learned that he's right.

My zeal put my family on the defensive. They threw up walls that took years to break down. I didn't have the moral authority to challenge their beliefs or their lives. At that point, all I had was a new talk that my walk had yet to match up to.

Spending some time to develop as a disciple is a great thing. We need to know what we believe and have some knowledge of God's Word and His ways before we are going to be good at making disciples. On the other hand, there is a real temptation to just hang out with other growing Christians and tell each other how great God is.

So what has to happen for a developing disciple, a D on our grid, to become an E…to start sharing his faith with others in addition to growing in the faith himself?

I believe that four factors, four drivers, have to be in place. We have to understand our marching orders, fertilize our gratitude, overcome fear, and delegate responsibility.

OUR MARCHING ORDERS—MAKE DISCIPLES

Jesus' last instruction to us before He went back to heaven and assumed His position at the right hand of the Father was incredibly simple: "Go and make disciples."

Go means be active, be intentional. When you're invited into a situation, when He shows you an opportunity, go!

Does that mean we are to just fire off indiscriminately? No, not at all. I believe that God wants us to ask Him for instructions: "What would You have me do?" Then act, follow orders, obey.

Often, there's not much time; the orders come in the wink of an eye. Someone asks you a serious spiritual question…you have to answer. Will you speak from your heart and talk about your faith, or will you wimp out and give some safe answer? God tells us to "always be prepared to give an answer to everyone who asks you to give the reason for the hope that you have" (1 Peter 3:15).

So, if we're willing to *go*, then how do we *make disciples*?

We model the Christian life by being a disciple, and we respond to the opportunity to help others to take their next step toward becoming a disciple.

That's it.

"But I don't have the gift of evangelism," you say.

Scripture teaches that spiritual gifts belong to God. They are given to us for a period of time to accomplish His purpose in that moment. We never take title to a spiritual gift; it's never ours, it's God's.

So when we are about our Father's business, we act in faith and courage. We obey. We do what He told us to do, with the best of our talents and abilities. If He needs to lend us a spiritual gift to accomplish what He wants to accomplish, that's up to Him. I'm to do what I'm supposed to do; He will fill in the gap between my abilities and His desired outcome.

FERTILIZE OUR GRATITUDE

As I said back in chapter 2, gratitude is a great motivator. When we start to consider sharing our faith, it's good to think back on all that God has done for us.

During a series of messages on evangelism, our pastor had us think back to the person who was most influential in our becoming a Christian. We were challenged to write a thank-you letter to that person, sharing the good things God has done in our lives since we made that commitment to Him.

As I reflected on all the blessings that have come my way since that night in 1983, I thought, "Why in the world would I hesitate to share Christ with someone? I could be the catalyst for that person having the same kind of blessings that I've had."

The person I wrote my letter to taught me an incredible principle that I rely on almost daily: *The only sure cure for anxiety is a grateful heart.* When I hesitate, get anxious, or start to chicken out in being public about my faith, I regain my confidence by thinking back on what God has done for me. The more I reflect on His goodness to me, the more guts I have to be bold—not in jamming my faith down someone's throat, but in making sure that God is given the spotlight in every aspect of what I do. The more grateful I am, the more courageous I become.

OVERCOME FEAR

We Christians have the greatest product in the world, but there is this wall, this fear, that shuts us down and shuts us up. Questions flood our minds and hearts, thoughts such as:

- "Yes, I love God, and He's given me a wonderful life, but I'm just not sure about what I'm supposed to do about this 'sharing my faith' thing."
- "That's just not me."
- "I'm a Calvinist. If God is going to save the folks at work, then He'll do it with or without me."
- "They'll think I'm stupid. I know so little Scripture."
- "How far do I go? How much do I say? When will they turn on me?"
- "The last thing I want to do is mess this up. They've finally gotten interested in Christianity, and I'm supposed to be the one to help them?"
- "I'm not there yet. I'm no saint. I'm just not ready."
- "I would be so embarrassed. I'm no role model. I've got no business talking about Christianity."
- "What if she gets mad? I have to work with her."
- "He'll think I'm just another Bible thumper and tune me out. I know he will."

All of these objections flow from fear—fear of what others will think, fear of failure, fear of rejection, and fear of embarrassment. I feel like an expert on fear, because fear is what kept me from selling out to Christ until I was thirty-three years old. These very fears are what robbed me of more than twenty years that I could have enjoyed walking with my heavenly Father.

I've learned one huge fact about fear, and it applies to all of the fears I just mentioned. Behind every fear is a lie. Let me explain.

Behind every fear is a lie.

Second Timothy 1:7 says, "For God has not given us a spirit of fear, but of power and of love and of a sound mind" (NKJV).

I now know that when I am feeling fear, it is *not* coming from God. That really helps me. If I can identify the source of a problem, then I'm a long way down the road toward solving it.

To know that fear is not coming from inside me helps also. Since Jesus Christ is living inside me, and where the light is the darkness cannot be, fear has to be external. It has to be coming from somewhere else.

So if fear isn't coming from God, and it's not coming from inside me, where is it coming from? The spirit of fear comes from the evil one: Fear is a child of the father of lies. Lies such as, "You're going to mess this up," for example. When I'm following orders from God and He is involved, there is no way I can mess up.

Take every one of the fearful questions that the enemy fires off at our minds when we are about to take a stand for Jesus Christ, and you'll find a lie buried behind the fear. Let's look at a few of them:

- *"Yes, I love God, and He's given me a wonderful life, but I'm just not sure about what I'm supposed to do about this 'sharing my faith' thing."*
  FEAR: Failure
  LIE: It's not really important for you to share your faith.
  GOAL OF THE LIE: To confuse you so that you won't do or say anything

- *"That's just not me"*
  FEAR: Embarrassment

LIE: You'll look stupid in front of your friends if you speak up.
GOAL OF THE LIE: To keep you prideful and paralyze you so that you'll stay quiet

* *"They'll think I'm stupid. I know so little Scripture."*
FEAR: That people will think badly of you
LIE: They'll think you're one of those brainless fanatics; you don't even know what you believe.
GOAL OF THE LIE: To keep you bound up in your own deal so you won't start sharing with others

* *"How far do I go? How much do I say? When will they turn on me?"*
FEAR: Rejection
LIE: You'll alienate your friends if you talk about your faith.
GOAL OF THE LIE: To keep you silent and keep them from hearing about Christ from someone who might have great credibility and influence

* *"The last thing I want to do is mess this up. They've finally gotten interested in Christianity and I'm supposed to be the one to help them?"*
FEAR: Inadequacy
LIE: You aren't good enough, and besides, someone else can do this better than you.
GOAL OF THE LIE: To keep you looking for someone else to do it rather than to step up yourself

Overcoming these fears begins with recognizing the source. I can deal with fear when I know that it's coming from the evil one and that its purpose is to thwart what God would have me do. I'm just not going to let that happen. God has given me a spirit of love and of power and of a sound mind. So trusting that God is for me and with me, I just wade into whatever I'm afraid of, knowing that I'm on a mission from God, that He is for me, that He is there with me, and most importantly, that I'm not responsible for the outcome.

Here are two good ways of dealing with fear. First, ask, "What's the worst that can happen?" If it goes really badly, what does that look like? Usually, we'll see that the worst outcome of sharing our faith isn't a bad thing at all. In our culture, we don't get put in jail or executed. We aren't likely to get fired. Usually, the worst thing that can happen is that someone will smile at us and politely tell us they're not interested in what we have to say. Now how bad can that be?

Second, we can deal with fear by focusing on the upside: "What is the best thing that can happen if I take this risk?" When I consider that God could use me to help bring someone into His family, it's humbling. If I think that I could be talking to the mother or father of the next Billy Graham or the next Mother Teresa, it's even more awesome.

With God, all things are possible. We never know what blessings wait for us if we will just do the next thing that He puts in front of us, and not chicken out.

We never know what blessings wait for us if we will just do the next thing that He puts in front of us.

DELEGATING RESPONSIBILITY FOR THE OUTCOME

My fear level goes down significantly when I remember that I'm not responsible for the outcome of my actions, just for doing the next right thing to the best of my ability. Again, I fall back on the promise that Scripture provides. We know that it's His will for all to come to know Him (2 Peter 3:9), and we know that no one will come to Him unless the Father draws him to Himself (John 6:44).

Now I don't pretend to know how to square up these two promises. What I do know is that it's God's job to work it all out, not mine. I am to simply tell people my story; I point people to the Scriptures that He calls to my mind; I share the resources He has put into my control and pray for the people I'm involved with. If they trust Jesus Christ, then I've done my job. If they reject Christ, then I've done my job. If they procrastinate and never get around to making a decision, then I've still done my job.

So the Developing D has only to continue to grow in his intimacy with God and to actively connect with other Christians. But to move to full obedience to God, there's one more step, one more level of commitment required.

Becoming an Excelling E brings it all together.

COUNTING OUR SOLDIERS

The Excelling E's

FINALLY, WE GET TO THE EASY ONES...THE ACTIVE, GROWING, public Christians that we work with, the people who care about bringing others to Christ in the workplace. These are the names you wrote in column E on your intentionality map. These are the folks who are fighting the good fight alongside you. They are about our Father's business full-time.

These are people like Jim Lyons, an obstetrician who has delivered more than five thousand babies over his thirty-eight-year career. But Jim can be spotted at coffee shops all around the city, meeting with guys and helping them move to the next step in their faith. At any given time, Jim will be meeting with as many as twenty-five different people, sharing his experience, sharing his wisdom, sharing his faith. He's an Excelling E of the highest order.

Excelling Christians have welded their life purpose to their work purpose. They are fully integrated. While they do their secular jobs (and do them well), they have a spiritual purpose every day. They are on a mission from God, and it's all wrapped in with what they do for a living. As a friend of mine said recently, "I'm still in business and always will be, but the work is fulfilling only when it's got a God-purpose to it." That's where the work and spiritual worlds mesh, when we "work at it with all [our] heart, as working for the Lord, not for men" (Colossians 3:23). That's an Excelling E—fully effective in what he does for a living and fully effective as an ambassador for the Lord Jesus Christ.

Excelling Christians have welded their life purpose to their work purpose.

But if your list is like mine, you didn't need a second sheet of paper to conclude your list of E's. There aren't that many Jim Lyonses out there. Too many of us have hidden. We haven't compromised what we believe; we've just gone undercover. We've become secret agents for God.

Now don't get me wrong. There are some visible Christians out there in the marketplace. The sign carriers, for instance, are intent on leading people to Jesus, and there's no question about them being active or intentional. They are after it. They want everyone to be saved and they want them saved now.

The sign carriers that you know, everyone else at work knows. They have fish stickers, fish pins, and fish symbols on their cars. They let everyone know what they believe and why. People that I have worked with call them Bible thumpers. These are the folks who have helped turn the words "born again" from a description of a spiritual event to a demeaning name assigned to any active Christian. Although it may be unintentional, these well-meaning Christians often come across as self-righteous and judgmental. "I've got it; you don't. You need it, and I want to give it to you." The problem is that "it" isn't very attractive to people in our culture when "it" is perceived to be a holier-than-thou brand of Christianity.

You may be one of those people. If you are, and God has led you to do the things that you do, God bless you and Godspeed. But I have seen a built-in resistance to Christians who approach their fellow workers and their workplace this way.

The Excelling E's that you want to find are people like John Dobbs. No one I've met has modeled this concept better than John. John was an employee at InterServ, our second start-up venture. He was also a committed Christian. Although he was a lower-level manager in the fulfillment operation, John always performed as if the company's survival depended on him. But what really made everyone appreciate him was his genuine concern for the other people in the company. He was never patronizing or intruding. But whenever someone had a need, he always seemed to have the margin in his life to accommodate them. And when the opportunity presented itself, he managed to make known the source of his inner joy and peace.

In my effort to approach my workplace as a venue for having influence for Jesus Christ, I couldn't help noticing that John was doing the same thing. Eventually, we talked about our mutual efforts. Once aware of our common goal, we were able to keep each other posted on our progress. On several occasions, my wife and I committed to pray for John's success with some of the people he was reaching at work. Likewise, I began to share with the same people when the opportunity arose. And whenever there was a breakthrough, we would let each other know and celebrate together.

Eventually, two key people in the company came to faith in Jesus Christ. And these were high-level executives, far removed from John's day-to-day role in the company. But John played a significant part in the process. One of the men had been completely turned off to God. The other had attended church, but had been mad at God since an early age. Over time, our efforts to expose them to the truth of God's Word paid off. I've even had the privilege of watching both of them mature to the point of sharing their faith and reproducing it in others as well.

BINOCULARS, ANYONE?

So how do you spot an E? Are they C's on steroids? Do you just look for the perfect attendance pins from Sunday school on the lapel? (Just kidding. I know that no one wears lapels anymore.)

So how do you spot an E? Are they C's on steroids?

E's are going to be found leading and doing. They will be the best workers, the most respected leaders, the most loved and cherished among their peers. Why? Because Jesus Christ inhabits their lives and hearts, and He is irresistible and irrepressible when He is given the controls in a person's life. Understand, we are all works in process, but there is something different about a person when they have embraced Christ at this level. They are characterized by peace, love, joy, patience, kindness, goodness, faithfulness, gentleness, and self-control. When you think of the people you listed in column E of your IMAP, do these words describe them?

When you find an employee-led Bible study, you'll often find an E in the leadership role. Similarly (but not always), E's are the people who head up various charity efforts and fundraisers for their churches and ministries. And they are the first on the scene to take meals to homes where loved ones have died or where people have been sick.

Remember, E's know and love God enough that they want to share Him with others. Gratitude first shows up when we become Christians. We become C's and begin to grasp God's love for us. D's go deeper and learn enough to be even more grateful for what Christ has done for them. But E's...their gratitude bucket is so full that it overflows. They act selflessly; they give of their time, money, and effort with no expectation of getting anything in return. They realize that giving is really receiving, and that true joy comes when we emulate Jesus in everything we do.

Another way to spot E's is by their books. E's are always lending or giving away copies of *Mere Christianity* by C. S. Lewis, *The Case for Christ* and *The Case for Faith* by Lee Strobel, *The Purpose-Driven Life* by Rick Warren, and books by Josh McDowell and Ravi Zacharias. These books are tools in their toolkits to lend or give to people when they show interest in spiritual things or have questions about Christianity.

E's can be spotted because they are on purpose. They have intentionality. They aren't just floating along, waiting to give a defense of their faith. They are active, observant initiators who constantly look for the right time to show love and to explain where their love comes from.

WHY HANG OUT WITH E'S?

When I was first promoted to a sales manager position many years ago, my boss taught me a principle that has stuck with me. "Spend time with your strongest and your weakest people." His theory was that you will learn stuff from your top performers that you can use to help your middle and lower performers. And at the same time, you encourage these excellent performers to keep on keeping on...to keep hitting home runs.

Andy is a good friend of mine who happens to be an Excelling E. One day he was talking about his friend Pete who had just become a Christian. I asked how that came about. Andy said, "Well, I asked him if he would study the Bible with me. He said yes and we dug into the book of John. After a few months, he decided that Jesus really is who He says He is."

"And Pete, a nonbeliever, agreed to study the Bible with you?" I asked, somewhat in disbelief.

"Yes."

I thought, *Wow!* Then I started thinking about Craig.

I had been meeting and talking to Craig for a number of years. (He claims that we had more than five hundred breakfasts together over his twelve-year search for truth.) We had first met when he was a young sales rep in my first company. He had blossomed professionally, getting promoted several times, and eventually moved on to start his own company.

Craig was an Apathetic A when we first got to know each

other. Like many of us, he had a really bad turnoff with church at a young age. When his best friend was killed by a reckless driver at age seventeen, Craig decided that he wanted no part of God.

Over the years though, God continued to work on Craig. He developed an insatiable curiosity about spiritual things. Still stiff-arming God, Craig would read a book a week. He went with me to Promise Keepers, to the Billy Graham Crusade, and to the High Tech Prayer Breakfast several times. But he couldn't let go of his old resentment toward God. He had become a solid Beginning to Search B…and I was sure that he was going to die there of old age.

But when I nervously asked him to study the Bible with me, he shocked me by saying yes. As Andy had done with Pete, I suggested we study the book of John. We studied a chapter a week, and I made up a couple of questions to direct his attention to the meat of each chapter. Craig accepted Jesus Christ the week we studied John 17.

If I hadn't gotten the stimulation from another E, I would never have ventured into studying the Bible with Craig.

E'S ARE YOUR BEST RESOURCE

No doubt about it, other E's are my best source of ideas on how to help people move from column to column. They are also my best source of resources to tap into. With thousands of Christian books coming out every year, there is no way that any one person can read them all. But E's are always reading new stuff, looking for ways to improve their game. Having a group of E's that you can partner with gives you leverage.

Other E's are my best source of ideas on how to help people move from column to column.

There are so many great communicators in the church today. Having partners who attend different churches gives you a living catalog of talks and sermons to share with people. I've started cataloging the sermons I heard using A through E so that I can recommend an appropriate message to other E's when I know they are facing a particular situation with someone in their sphere of influence.

Recently, Charlie and Bob were preparing to fly to visit an old friend who is terminally ill. They were pretty sure that Mark was not a Christian, but had found him to be open to talking about spiritual things when they had been on the phone with him. (Most of us get more open to spiritual things when we enter the "valley of the shadow of death.")

How could I help them out with their mission? I remembered a CD that explains the gospel in straightforward terms. I thought, *If they don't get to have a conversation with Mark about the gospel, at least they can have a "leave behind" that he can listen to.* I also remembered a CD that encourages Christians to be courageous about sharing their faith.

I took the CDs to Charlie's house and left them in his mailbox late on the night before he and Bob were to leave. I left instructions for each of the CDs. I suggested they hold on to the first one and leave it behind only if it didn't work out to discuss salvation directly with Mark. I asked them to listen to the second one in the rental car as they drove to Mark's house.

What happened? I don't know yet. You see, it's not about outcomes; it's about obedience. I prayed for Charlie and Bob and the ideas for helping equip them came to me. I dug out the sermon CDs and delivered them. I did what God led me to do. They did what God led them to do. The outcome is up to God.

Often another E will have access to someone on your IMAP list that you don't have.

Joe showed up at our Friday Bible study every now and then. Joe loved to hunt and fish...loved it passionately. Only one other guy in the group, Lane, was passionate about hunting. Joe and Lane got hooked up and went on a trip together, and Joe prayed to receive Jesus Christ out there in the woods. (Lane jokingly claims that the presence of guns may have had more to do with Joe's decision than the presence of God.)

But you see, I would never have had that conversation with Joe. I'm not a hunter. But knowing other E's—knowing their interests, hobbies, passions, personalities, and life stories—gives me an army of soldiers that I can call on. Conversely, since I am a business guy, I get called on regularly to meet with people from the business world whose frame of reference I understand. E's are teammates, all working together to help people find Truth.

Knowing other E's gives me an army of soldiers that I can call on.

The beauty of the IMAP process is that you are meeting people exactly where they are, and you're focused only on helping them move one step closer. It's a lot easier to develop a strategy to help someone move one step than it is to lead them to Christ. And other E's will be your best source of advice on strategies and tactics.

E IS ALSO FOR ENCOURAGEMENT

The other huge value of identifying fellow soldiers is the encouragement that E's can be to each other. In his book *The Journey of Desire*, John Eldredge says of his friend Brent, "Our friendship was a shared journey, a mutual quest for the secret of our souls. It took us...into the desperate battle raging all around for the hearts of others as well."[6]

It can be lonely out there. When your business isn't doing very well, you need a shoulder. You need to be able to share with a brother how you're feeling, not just about your spiritual pursuits but about your work, your job situation, and even your future. When you ask him to pray for you, you know that he will.

And when major opportunities for truth sharing come up, you can call another E, tell him about the conversation you're about to have, and he will drop whatever he's doing and pray for you. He knows how important what you are doing is...that someone's eternal destination is at stake, not to mention the quality of the rest of that person's life on earth.

The common mission of E's opens up a whole new depth of relationship between them. There is nothing more important than the mission to be about my Father's business. Both my autonomy and my privacy are secondary to the mission. So it's not just okay but welcomed when my friend Tut asks me, "How are you doing with the Lord?" It's fine when I ask my friend

Andy, "What's the question that you hope I don't ask you today?" And it's not a surprise when I ask my friend David, "How's it going with your IMAP people? Are you making any progress with Mark?" That accountability helps me keep focused on the important things, not just the urgent ones.

Excelling for Christ...that's where we want to be. We've got Him in our minds and hearts, we're growing in Him every day, and we're giving Him away to others.

SENSING THE SENSITIVITIES

THERE IS A MOVEMENT OF GOD IN THE MARKETPLACE. Literally thousands of executives and business owners are beginning to think about how they can make a difference for Christ in their workplace. Bible study groups are being formed, prayer groups are coming together, and organizations are taking on ministry and charity projects left and right.

Top Christian leaders and thinkers from Billy Graham to Henry Blackaby have talked about it. There have been articles in every major newspaper and cover stories in *Newsweek* and *Time* magazines. Workplace ministry is hot.

But as with so many movements, the worst enemies of progress often come from within. Some people become so zealous that they overstep their bounds and bring down the wrath of those opposed to the movement.

For years, pro-life activists made real progress in raising the country's awareness of the moral and ethical issues surrounding abortion. Then, a small number of radical people started bombing abortion clinics and killing doctors. The movement lost momentum, hindered by the very people who most wanted to see it succeed.

Where are the land mines for us as workplace ministers? What could we do, acting with the best of intentions, that could hurt the cause of Christ at work? What do we need to be sensitive to so that we don't limit our influence or, even worse, cause the organizations that we work for to step in and inhibit our kingdom efforts?

Most of the concepts that I have talked about relate to individuals, to the one-on-one relationships that we develop at work. And because of that focus, the sensitivities that come to the fore are personal ones...things that we have to be aware of in any relationship. But there are other sensitivities that become relevant only in a corporate or organizational setting. These are different and require a bit of caution in how we approach them. Let's talk about both.

RELATIONSHIPS REQUIRE CARE

As I mentor young men each year, one word becomes the theme word, and that word is almost always *careful*. Be careful with people. They are sensitive. They listen more than you think, and they listen to more than your words.

Be careful with people. They are sensitive.

For years, I placed a high premium on being funny. I was the king of one-liners. I always had a wisecrack to offer, regardless of where I was or who I was with. As I matured, I began to notice that not everyone was laughing, particularly my wife. She began to help me see that I didn't always know where other people were coming from—what was in their past, what they were going through. I could be hurting people with my attempts at humor…the very people God called me to have influence with.

With the onslaught of homosexuality into our culture, very few families have not been affected by someone "coming out." So making judgmental comments about gays or lesbians will almost always strike at the heart of someone who is connected to a person in the homosexual community. One off-the-wall comment, even if it's accurate or biblical, can build a wall between you and that person that will never come down. Your influence is over.

Other sensitive areas are more subtle.

With the divorce rate at near record levels, most every family has been touched by divorce. That means that many of us are growing up without dads in our homes. When we start talking about our heavenly Father, or even our own fathers, we can get onto sensitive ground without even knowing it.

Sexual abuse is an insidious curse that many people have to deal with as adults. Almost any discussion related to sex can set off emotions in someone who has been abused or who may be trying to overcome the consequences of abuse.

Ethnicity can be a much stronger dimension in people's lives than we realize. I thought nothing of being of Scottish decent until I was having dinner in London with a businessman and his wife, who was French. I quickly learned that traditional French people have two inherent characteristics: they hate the English and they love the Scots. This lady's whole countenance toward me changed when she finally heard my last name and realized my heritage. Comments about any nationality or race hold the potential to set off a response, whether positive or negative, toward us.

Religious heritage and denominational connections are another one. My next-door neighbors are committed evangelical Christians…who happen to also be Catholic. On occasion, we will be in a social situation together and someone will make a slanted reference to Catholics, to the pope, or to some of the sexual abuse scandals that have rocked the Catholic church. I can see the emotions go up and the defensiveness take hold. I think, *If they were Catholic by heritage but not Christians by belief, they would hear nothing else that person said.*

My friend Curt is a committed Excelling E. He is constantly scheduling Bible study groups and prayer groups in the conference room at the company where he works. He began to notice an unusual number of conflicts on the schedule for the room, so he asked his boss's secretary, who scheduled the room, what was going on. He learned, somewhat painfully, that she was Jewish and that she didn't take too well to this constant stream of Christian activity outside her office door. Curt was able to get the conference room scheduling task reassigned to someone else, but he got blindsided by an unknown sensitivity held by an important person in his sphere of influence.

Another sensitivity to be aware of relates to what people's grown-up kids believe. Parents tend to like what their kids like, to be open to whatever their kids are open to. When we start making comments about the Buddhist monks that we encountered at the airport, we could be in the presence of a parent whose son has become a Buddhist. While she may not believe as her son does, she may be protective and block you out if she perceives you to be judging her son.

BUILD THE BRIDGE FIRST

Another of my favorite sayings is, "Build a bridge between you and the other person that is strong enough to carry the weight of the gospel." Get to know people before you start telling stories and talking about potentially sensitive stuff.

Once people know you and *know your heart*, they're much less likely to take offense at things that you say. Getting to know someone takes time...lots of time. We get in a hurry, particularly when we are on a mission from God. As I said before, the mistakes I have made in trying to influence people for Christ have come from being too chicken or being in too big a hurry.

> Once people know you and know your heart, they're much less likely to take offense at things that you say.

Suppose you think you're ready to discuss spirituality with one of your vendor's representatives. Or you're ready to tell your coworker about your conversion to Christianity. Or imagine that you have a committed but passive Christian friend that you want to talk to about becoming an active Christian and starting to share his faith. How do you know that the time is right?

A good litmus test for where you stand in your relationship with a person is this question: *Am I certain that if I bring up this issue, the relationship will be secure, regardless of the answer?*

It's a gut-check question. If you have to think about it, the answer is no, and you shouldn't bring it up yet. You should continue to develop the relationship until the trust level is higher. When you can answer that question with an intuitive, unequivocal yes, then the bridge is strong enough to cross.

You see, the person has to value *you* more than he values his answer. If he feels threatened by what he's going to have to say to answer your question honestly, he will either have to lie (i.e., tell you what he thinks you want to hear), or he will tell you the truth, but with a finality that says, "I'm not going into that with you ever again."

When a person values you and his relationship with you, he will feel free to answer and won't feel threatened or embarrassed. If he is confident of your acceptance, then he won't feel at risk when he answers your question.

On the other hand, you have to be ready to *accept* that person's answer just as it comes...and without emotion. Don't try to sell him on your answer or your beliefs or your plan for his life. Just respond with an accepting smile. If the answer is anything less that what you want it to be, there will be disappointment in your heart, but you *must* not let that drive your response, because to do so communicates rejection.

Instead, celebrate a victory. You have been successful if you were able to broach a new subject, ask a question, get an honest answer, and keep the relationship intact. That is a victory in anyone's book.

Remember the old Chinese proverb: "A journey of a thousand miles begins with a single step." Don't be in a hurry. God isn't, and He is the one at work here. You're just doing your part...one step at a time.

CORPORATE AND ORGANIZATIONAL SENSITIVITIES

We've just worked through some common-sense rules for sensitivity in our one-on-one relationships. Now let's talk about some similar rules for being about our Father's business within an organization.

Surprisingly, there are very few rules that govern sharing our faith in the workplace. As employees, we have almost free rein to say whatever we want to other employees. Companies can impose their own workplace rules about talking on the job, use of telephones, conference rooms, e-mail, and so on, and as workplace Christians who are attempting to be model employees, we are to meet and exceed the expectations of our superiors on all of these policies. But from the standpoint of the law, sharing our faith at work is a basic right that you and I can exercise without fear.

> Sharing our faith at work is a basic right that you and I can exercise without fear.

When you are the boss, it's a little different matter. Two major rules come into play here: rules that prohibit religious *discrimination* and religious *harassment*.

Religion is one category of several covered by Title VII of the Civil Rights Act. The others include race, color, gender, and nationality. And religion includes atheism but not agnosticism. Go figure.

To avoid religious discrimination, we simply can't let someone's religious beliefs (or the lack thereof) influence who we hire, fire, or promote. Furthermore, we can't extend any benefits to one person that we don't extend to all employees, based on religion.

What does that mean? You are asking for trouble if you ask questions about someone's religious beliefs or heritage in the interview process. You just can't go there, which in my view is wonderful. It prevents Christian employers from creating holy huddles and makes it necessary for people like you and me to connect with new employees and build relationships with them.

You are also asking for trouble if you exclusively select Christians for promotions. Those you promote have to be the people who do the best job, who exhibit the best talent and commitment to excellence. If those leaders come from the ranks of the Christians, then so be it. But if people are promoted because they have good character or they best represent management's philosophies and values, then look out. The worker who doesn't come to the Bible study, who doesn't receive the morning devotional e-mail, and who gets passed over for the better job is going to come knocking on your door, or on the door of the Equal Employment Opportunity Commission.

If you are the boss, the manager, the CEO, or the business owner, you are considered to be a control person. Your activities become closely scrutinized when a disgruntled employee files a discrimination or harassment charge. The courts have deemed you to have a sort of conflict of interest when you have the power to hire, fire, pay, and promote *and* you are pressing your Christian agenda hard in the workplace.

So it bears repeating—when you're dealing with people one-on-one, be sure that the relationship is strong enough that you can lead them to the next step with Christ without fear that they will feel threatened and turn on you.

If you are in management, it's better to delegate the out-front roles to others in your organization. While it's not illegal for the boss to lead the Bible study, it may not be wise. Why make yourself a lightning rod for discrimination or harassment charges when there are others in the organization who may have more in common with the people they will be leading?

While hiring, firing, and promoting are obvious opportunities for us to wrongly reward Christians over non-Christians, benefits are a little less obvious. These can include time off to attend religious activities, books and publications that others don't get, and even food while attending religious events.

My friend Craig Eddy provides a lunch for his employees when they come to his weekly Route 66 sessions. Those who attend watch DVDs of praise bands and then watch a DVD sermon by a great Christian communicator. The session ends with a prayer; then everyone goes back to work.

Since that time off is during lunch and everyone gets the same amount, no problem. But what about the food? Since the food could be construed as a benefit, Craig provides the same lunch to every employee who wants it, whether they come to Route 66 or not. That's wise, and it keeps him and his company completely within the letter and the spirit of the law.

Harassment is the other big scary word that gets batted

around in the workplace ministry arena. Like discrimination, harassment is pretty much in the eye of the beholder, but there are some clear guidelines that might help.

Imagine that everyone in your work world was red—their skin, their hair, their clothes, everything about them…red. Now, imagine that you are blue. All day long, you stand out; everyone knows that you're different.

We all want to belong, to be accepted, to fit in somehow. When you're the only one that's blue, you don't fit. They are in; you are out. Even though you may have the same job and be treated the same way, you will start to feel the eyeballs, you'll notice the conversations that you aren't included in, you'll take note of every little decision, looking for telltale evidence that you've been singled out, that you aren't getting the same deal as all the red people.

That is the genesis of religious harassment charges—people who aren't believers are made to feel out rather than in.

Companies are wise to develop and post carefully written policies to avoid making religious belief an implicit requirement for being a part of the company. Policies also need to be developed and published stating that the company doesn't discriminate in hiring, promotion, and benefits based on religious belief. That's a minimum.

In many small companies, these policies may be the only written ones that exist, but they should exist if you plan to be both public and intentional about living out your faith at work. As the old saying goes, "an once of prevention is worth a pound of cure."

Policies regarding use of company facilities, including conference rooms, bulletin boards, and e-mail systems, have to specify equal access for all religious groups. That's really a tough one if an employee who belongs to a cult asks if he can use the conference room. But turning him down could be just the setup he's been looking for to file a charge against your company. I take you back to 2 Timothy 1:7: "For God has not given us a spirit of fear, but of power and of love and of a sound mind" (NKJV). So what if someone holds a meeting of their cult group in your conference room? Let them use it, but pray against it (in private, of course). This is a long-term effort; don't let the small stuff trip you up.

But the proof of the pudding comes in how the organization operates every day. If there are Bible studies or prayer groups, make sure that attendance is *truly* optional—that failure to attend will not affect advancement in the company. Supervisors have to be trained to *not* come up to employees who didn't attend a Bible study and say, "Where were you this morning?" Or, "We've been missing you at the prayer group." Again, if the relationship is there and is dependable, no problem. But when a person in authority is construed as pressing someone to attend a religious function, you're set up for a harassment charge.

> When a person in authority is construed as pressing someone to attend a religious function, you're set up for a harassment charge.

If meetings open in prayer, make it clear to employees that they don't have to participate or that they can arrive late, after the prayer.

Being sure that you understand what is and is not off-limits will give you great confidence as you go about our Father's business. As I have researched these issues over the years, I have been surprised by how much freedom employees, business leaders, and owners have to be active in their faith at work. There are very few constraints, so long as we use good judgment and common sense.

WELL DONE! THAT'S WHAT I WANT TO HEAR

My mother-in-law, a saint of a woman, recently passed away at age ninety-four. I sat by her bed just a few days before she died and asked, "Grandma, what would you like on your tombstone?"

With no hesitation, she said, "Well done."

Aren't those the words you want said about you, if not on your tombstone, from God when you meet Him face-to-face?

Those words would be so sweet to hear. Imagine how Jesus felt when He came up from His baptism and heard that voice say, "This is My beloved Son, in whom I am well pleased" (Matthew 3:17, NKJV). We have the opportunity to be greeted in heaven someday by that same voice, with those ultimate affirming words.

In these pages, I have shared an approach to life that takes the great commission seriously. To get up every morning focused on influencing specific people toward Christ would be a huge change for most people. It's a tall order, I know.

To get up every morning focused on influencing specific people toward Christ would be a huge change for most people.

If you take my challenge, you're going to have highs and lows. There will be times when you *know* that God used you. You will see people's lives change. You'll see that fruit start to emerge in their lives, and you'll know that you played a little part in making it happen. You may see their kids go in a better direction. You realize that your involvement may have shaped a third and fourth generation. Years from now, lives will be richer and kids will grow up stronger because of what you did to influence your workmates for Jesus Christ.

There will also be times when you think "What's the use?" Things won't happen the way you want them to. People won't respond to your love. You'll get rejected and you'll feel like a failure.

What's worse is that sometimes you will completely forget to be about your Father's business. There will be days, even weeks, when making disciples will just not show up on your radar screen. You'll get distracted with kids, with work, with houses, with life. You'll just forget.

When I read the Old Testament, I'm baffled by how the children of Israel could have experienced such dramatic, direct intervention from God and then forgot Him just a short time later. Then I look at how I live my life and I understand—I'm just like them. I've seen His miraculous hand in my life, and then I get completely self-focused. I just forget.

If you're like that too, please don't give up. Whenever you realize that you've forgotten, just get back at it. Take out your IMAP and ask God where He would have you go. You'll find that He has been right there, waiting for you to get back in the game.

This work, this kingdom work, will never be complete. That's the beauty of it. You've always got a job, an important job, and the Boss is always happy to see you back at work, no matter how long you've been laying out. There are no layoffs, no mandatory retirement age, and no pay cuts. The job is totally portable, available to you wherever you live, anywhere in the world. You are not responsible for results, just for showing up. There are no goals, no quotas, and no targets to hit. It's an awesome opportunity.

So let's give it a shot. Let's be about our Father's business!

A FINAL WORD

THIS BOOK HAS LAID OUT A PROCESS THAT CAN HELP YOU organize your efforts to influence others for Christ in the workplace. As I developed the intentionality map over the years, it became evident to me that reaching out to those in our sphere of influence is what we are supposed to do all the time, in every context, with everyone that we care about. It's not just about the people we work with, it's about the people in every arena and compartment of our lives.

I went back and reworked my IMAP. I added my wife, my kids, my sister and brother, and their spouses and children. I added my neighbors and my friends from church and from previous companies where I worked. Everyone that I care about personally is on my IMAP grid.

Everyone that I care about personally is on my IMAP grid.

Now, the columns got a lot longer, but the picture also got a lot clearer. I have a spiritual job to do both at the office and in other places. I have more people to pray for, more people to intentionally interact with, and more requirements on my time. But I believe that my life, my work, and my ministry are far more integrated now than ever before.

Oddly enough, God still gives me about the same number of assignments each day as He did before I expanded my lists. I pray for each person less frequently than I did before, but God knows my heart and He still calls my attention to just the right ones when I give Him the opportunity to instruct me.

Ready? Ready to be about your Father's business?

There's no better life!

STUDY GUIDE FOR PERSONAL REFLECTION OR SMALL GROUP DISCUSSION

YOU ARE ABOUT TO EMBARK ON ONE OF THE MOST SIGNIFICANT journeys you will ever take: making your work into something that is God-centered. It's huge! It can make every day an adventure, every relationship a positive challenge, and every encounter with someone at work an opportunity.

Most of us work at a job every day. Most Americans who are physically able and who either have to or choose to, work. A small percentage can afford to retire or to work only part time.

So since we were designed by our Creator to work, and most of us do it, why are so few of us happy and fulfilled in our work? The secret lies in why we go to work. Six weeks from now, we'll have a clear answer to the "why" question as well as a process that will help us to know "how" as well.

We'll begin by looking at our workplace and how we know that we're supposed to take on two jobs at the same time: the job that brings in a paycheck *and* the job that Jesus gave us when He said, "Go make disciples."

Our next priority will be to examine ourselves and see what we need to do to become useful as a "special agent" for God in the "work nation." One of our first looks will be into the mirror. Where am I in my spiritual life? What's my story? Am I ready and willing to tell it to the people that I work with?

Then we'll explore ways to effectively interact with the people in our workplace for the purpose of influencing them toward Christ. We'll dig into the Scriptures to see what God has to say about our interactions with others, and we'll examine the model for our behavior, Jesus Christ, and how He interacted with people in His sphere of influence. And we'll finish by exploring what it looks like to be a fully devoted Christ follower who is growing in the faith and even reaching out to share Jesus with others.

That's what we'll be exploring over the next six weeks. What am I supposed to do? Where do I fit in? How do I change what I do from nine to five each day to make a difference for Christ?

There is no greater encouragement, no sense of fulfillment, nothing more enjoyable than knowing what God has called you to do. And then to know that you're doing it. That sounds pretty good! Let's go firm it up.

WEEK ONE: WORK, CALLING, AND THE NEXT STEP IN THE PURPOSE-DRIVEN LIFE

Read pages 13–30 in *About My Father's Business*.

Principles and Truths for This Week

1. Christianity is both a blessing and a calling. When we stop with the blessing—what we'll call phase-one or the I-focused part of Christianity—we miss the calling

and the opportunity to have true purpose and meaning in life, which comes with others-focused
Christianity ("phase two").

2. All Christians are called to make disciples. It's not
someone else's job.

3. Work is our assigned mission field; it's not second class,
and it's no less sacred a calling than being a pastor.

4. The purpose-driven life is about glorifying God. We
must do that at work by:

   a. being His.

   b. being respected.

   c. being intentional.

Memory Verse for Week One

In the same way, let your light shine before men, that
they may see your good deeds and praise your Father
in heaven.

MATTHEW 5:16

Rate Yourself (Be Kind!)

If you were sitting in a conference room and the speaker asked
you to take out a piece of paper and rate yourself from 1 to 10
as an evangelist or as a disciple maker, how would you rate
yourself? 10? 5? 2?

Most of us would have a hard time giving ourselves high
marks. To begin with, the bar has been set so high that we don't
feel that we could ever jump over it. We've heard about the guy
who leads people to Christ on airplanes, and he does it one after
another. We've never done that and have no vision for how we
ever could.

We've also defined *evangelism* wrongly. We think of it as an event rather than a process. And since we have no skill or experience in making those events happen, we feel bad about ourselves and withdraw from the process altogether.

Over the next few weeks, we want to clear up those wrong perceptions. Influencing people toward Christ is a process, not an event. It's a team effort in which many people play small roles that, together, have a huge impact. And just being on the team and being involved may be the most satisfying and fulfilling part of being a Christian. The process that we're going to learn will make evangelism and discipleship doable for you! Instead of seeing it as a source of frustration and feeling like a failure, you are going to get excited and energized about making a difference for Christ in the work nation.

The instruction that Jesus gave to "go and make disciples of all nations" (Matthew 28:19) is one that we've all heard. Some of us have glossed over verses like this one, assuming they were directed to someone else at some other time in some other place. Other people have a full load of guilt on their backs, knowing that the words were spoken by Jesus and directed to them, but they've never acted on the instruction, never tried to make a disciple, and never shared their faith with anyone, ever. In between these two extremes fall the rest of us. We "sort of" know that we're supposed to make disciples; we "sort of" know what that means, and we "sort of" try to, now and again, but we don't know what we're doing and we don't think we're very good at it. This week, we're going to get clear and specific about our calling to make disciples.

And Just What Is a Disciple?
A learner and follower of Jesus Christ! When we are about our

Father's business, we are learners and followers of Jesus Christ and we are intentional about leading others to be disciples also. Jesus' instruction was clear and specific, spoken after His resurrection, and recorded by all four of the gospel writers as well as the writer of the book of Acts.

Read each of the following verses. Record the instruction that Jesus gave in each verse below.

Matthew 28:19 _____

Mark 16:15 _____

Luke 24:47 _____

John 20:21 _____

Acts 1:8 _____

"Go and make" says "initiate," to start a creative process within someone—a process that will create a disciple! "All nations" includes our work nation. It's a place with its own culture, its own rules and laws, its own language, and even its own social order. We are to initiate the process that will create disciples in the work nation, just as a missionary to a foreign country would.

"Baptizing" indicates a rebirth. Leading people to rebirth is a part of "repentance and forgiveness of sins." "Preaching" says we intentionally communicate for the purpose of salvation. "Being sent" confirms that there is a "sender." We have a Master who is sending us, and we are obeying that Master, not just coming up with good things to do for God. And "be my witnesses" says that we must simply tell people what we have seen ourselves—what we have seen Jesus do in our own lives. Finally, "to the ends of the earth" certainly includes our work environment, which is the focus of this study.

The Work Nation Is Our Nation

Like it or not, work is its own nation of sorts. Only recently have Christians begun to see that this work nation is ripe for the gospel, and that we who journey there every day have a golden opportunity to influence that nation for Christ.

Our Paying Job

Regardless of our position or industry, we all are workers. Because work is hard, most of us think of it as a curse, something to be endured. But that isn't biblical truth. Check out Genesis 2:15:

> "The LORD God took the man and put him in the
> Garden of Eden to work it and take care of it."

Note that the fall of man didn't happen until later, in chapter 3, verse 6. And then in verse 17, when God is describing the consequences of man's rebellion against Him, He tells men that their work will now be "painful toil."

So work, in and of itself, isn't a curse. We were made to work. It is unnatural and debilitating to do nothing. Without work, we become like a fine car that never gets driven. We atrophy. We become a museum piece and we fall short of our intended purpose.

The key is to have *purpose* in our work—a reason to work in addition to simply earning money. To go further, it's actually a *more important* reason to work than earning money. It's an *eternal* reason!

Rick Warren's book *The Purpose Driven Life* convinces us that our purpose in life, including in our work life, is to glorify God. But how? How do we do that?

The word *glorify* can be interchanged with the word *praise*. God wants us to live our lives in such a way that we are a praise to Him. Whatever we do or say, however we act, wherever we go, our words and actions, even our thoughts are a praise to Him. He's proud of them, just as a dad is proud of every good word or action of his child.

Glorifying God with Our Lives

So how do we live a life that praises God every day at work? We're going to look at three fundamentals of a work life that praises God, and empowers us to "go and make disciples" (Matthew 28:19).

1. Be His. We must first ensure that we have been adopted into God's family and that we have a solid relationship with the Father. Read the section headed "Your Relationship with Christ" on pages 47–49 of this book and answer the following questions.

List three words that describe your life *before* you trusted Christ.

Describe, in three or four sentences, the circumstances that drove you to need the Lord in your life.

Again, in three or four sentences, detail what happened in the twenty-four hours surrounding your committing your life to Christ.

List three words that describe your life *since* you accepted God's offer of forgiveness through Jesus Christ.

What you have just written is the basic "skeleton" of your faith story—your testimony, to use a big church word. We'll come back to your story several times over the next weeks.

2. Be respected. If you decide to be about your Father's business in the workplace, you will only be effective if you are respected in the culture of the work nation. Just like any missionary assigned to carry Christ to another culture, you must know the "rules of the road" in that culture so that you can earn the respect of the people there, and ultimately gain influence with them. As usual, God has given us the answers to earning that respect in his Word. Read the following verses and learn nine keys to earning respect at work. Fill in each key on the line following the reference.

Proverbs 22:29 _____

Philippians 2:14 _____

Colossians 4:1 _____

Colossians 4:5–6 _____

1 Thessalonians 4:12 _____

Colossians 3:22–25 _____

Ecclesiastes 9:10 _____

Matthew 5:37 _____

Philippians 2:3–4 _____

"Now Daniel so distinguished himself among the administrators and the satraps by his exceptional qualities that the king planned to set him over the whole kingdom" (Daniel 6:3).

We will have limited influence at work for Christ unless we distinguish ourselves as great workers, as Daniel did. But if these qualities become descriptive of who we are at work, we can achieve great success in our jobs, and that will enable us to have influence as ministers as well!

3. Be intentional. When we first become committed Christians, we are giddy with our newfound faith and all the benefits of our new relationship with Christ.

"I have peace, I have forgiveness, I have purpose, I have a perfect Father who loves and protects me." "I have great new friends, I have a church, with people there who love me and care about me!" "I have the Bible...a dependable operator's manual for life." "I have a promise that I'll live forever in heaven." All true, and granted it's all good stuff!

But count how many I's are in that paragraph! It's all about me and what I get from God. This is what I call phase-one Christianity, and it's where most of us have stopped and camped out. It's why so many Christians and the churches they attend are so weak and lifeless.

Jesus calls us to phase-two Christianity. He wants us to make the move from me-centered Christianity to the others-centered life that He modeled for us.

Read Matthew 16:24 and answer the following:

1. If "anyone" comes after Jesus, where will he or she end up? Where is Jesus today?
2. How does the concept of denying yourself lie down with the "I" focus of phase-one Christianity?
3. What do you think "take up [your] cross" means?
4. How do you interpret "follow me" as it relates to the work nation?

Given the direct order to deny ourselves, take up our cross, and follow Him, we're not given the choice to just stay focused on ourselves. While it's comfortable to be quiet about our faith, to stay passive and to run and hide when issues come up at work, it's just not what Jesus told us to do.

So to be intentional means to move from passive to active, from phase-one Christianity, where it's all about *me,* to phase-two Christianity where it's about *others.* God wants us to place our focus on Him and on others. In Matthew 22:37–39, Jesus talked about this focus:

> "'Love the Lord your God with all your heart and with all your soul and with all your mind.' This is the first and greatest commandment. And the second is like it: 'Love your neighbor as yourself.'"

Intentionality means being on purpose in everything we do. We're focused on God all the time. We're constantly talking to Him, acknowledging His presence, thanking Him for what just happened, asking His advice on how to respond to the people and the situation at hand, asking Him for courage to take a risk, asking Him for the strength to stay in the game and not give up. We need His grace to accept people who aren't pulling their weight. We need His presence to willingly forgive the person who lied to us about something at work, even when that lie cost us something.

You see, intentionality is about motive, and God wants our motives to be about loving Him and about loving others. That's living a life that's a praise to Him in every dimension. That's self-lessness. That's being single-minded, with the focus of "all your heart," "all your soul," and "all your mind" being about Him.

Being about our Father's business adds a spiritual dimension to everything we do and to every work relationship. It says that we are to love and serve each person whom we encounter at work so that we can ultimately help him or her take the next step toward Christ, regardless of what that step is. We'll begin by getting to know our coworkers well enough that we discover what they believe. We'll pray for them and over time, God may just use us in some small way to influence them toward an exciting relationship with the Father.

So let's summarize what we've covered so far:

1. Being a disciple—a learner and follower of Jesus Christ—requires us to "go and make disciples" of others. Discipleship requires us to move beyond me-focused Christianity and into an others-focused life.

2. Our workplace is our "nation."

3. Our ability to make disciples at work hinges on three basics:

    a. that we are in fact Christians and that we ourselves have a personal relationship with Christ.

    b. that we go about our work life in a way that earns the respect of our coworkers, superiors, subordinates, suppliers, clients, and prospects.

    c. that we become intentional, in other words, "on purpose" in our work relationships for the purpose of influencing people toward Christ.

Questions for Discussion

1. Do you feel the "monkey"—the weight of responsibility to stand up for your faith—at your work? How do you respond to it?

2. Christians often live two lives: the Christian life at church and in Christian circles and then the other life that includes work and everything else. Where is your work life most disconnected from your church life?

3. Did you find it difficult to answer the questions in the section called "Be His?" Which question was the hardest to answer? Why?

4. For many, the idea that how we conduct ourselves at our work has a huge impact on our potential influence for Christ is a new one. Which of the nine attributes of a great worker is the biggest challenge for you? Why?

5. If you could get just one big thing out of the next six weeks, what would that be?

WEEK TWO: INTENTIONALITY

Read pages 30–55 in *About My Father's Business*.

Principles and Truths for This Week

1. God wants us to be intentional for Him as we go about our jobs.
2. We fail because we forget, we're afraid, and we don't connect with God as we go.
3. The motivation to be a disciple comes from a humble, surrendered heart, and that comes from brokenness and gratitude.
4. God has special blessings for those who follow Him into discipleship.
5. Discipleship is all about relationships.

Memory Verse for Week Two

But seek first his kingdom and his righteousness, and all these things will be given to you as well.

MATTHEW 6:33

Two Jobs

Isn't it strange how our jobs never quite satisfy us? Year after year, in survey after survey, we see that between 70 and 90 percent of Americans are dissatisfied with their jobs. Sure we have good days, and even seasons when things go well, but most of us feel that we are underemployed. We know we could handle bigger responsibilities if someone would just trust us and give us the chance. Many of us are burned out in our work, just going through the motions to earn a paycheck.

But what if we got up every day knowing that we were on a mission from God? What if we knew that what we were going to do today mattered, and mattered for all of eternity? What if I knew that I was the only person in the world who could do the job that I am called to do today? Would I feel needed? significant? fulfilled?

Well, that's the job you have—right now! It is no accident that you are where you are, doing what you are doing in your work. God has assigned you to be His special agent to whatever company or business you're working for.

Being about my Father's business means that as I do that paying job every day, I am also on a mission for God's invisible kingdom to the people with whom I come in contact in my work nation. I have my job as supervisor, account executive, or associate, but I also have my job as special agent for God at the same time. Generally, I'm a secret agent! But occasionally I have to break out and be public about who I work for and what I'm all about. This special-agent job is the job of being Jesus Christ's disciple. The challenge is put to us in Matthew 6:33. Read the verse and answer these questions.

What does He want us to "seek" first?

What does "and his righteousness" mean?

Where does His "kingdom" exist?

What does "all these things will be given to you as well" refer to?

So a paraphrase of Matthew 6:33 might say, "Make it your first job (seek first) to be about building My kingdom (in the hearts of men and women). As you do it, don't forget to seek My righteousness yourself, and I will meet the physical needs (all these things) of life for you."

The challenge is clear. Christ wants us to pursue the hearts of the people whom we encounter at work. *He wants us to be about the Father's business at work.*

Now that might have been interpreted a bit differently a few years back. In the traditional view of evangelism in the workplace, we might have thought that being a special agent for God meant that you had to:

- have a Bible on your desk.
- distribute gospel tracts to coworkers, clients, and prospects.
- press everyone you met to go to church (preferably yours!).
- wear crosses or Christian jewelry or display Christian symbols in your workspace and on your car.
- start or at least attend a company Bible study.
- memorize and be ready to give a presentation of the gospel, the Four Spiritual Laws, or something similar.

- be ready to lead a coworker through the "sinner's prayer."
- ask every person in your sphere of influence a litmus question such as, "If you died tonight, where would you spend eternity?" And if the answer was the incorrect one, you'd share the gospel and lead the person in the sinner's prayer immediately.
- pray for those who refuse to accept the gospel.

These are all good things, no doubt. But for many of us, they're just "not me." And we've learned that sometimes these very things can build walls instead of bridges between us and our unbelieving colleagues.

Here's a different list of things you might see a special agent for God doing at work. See which list sounds more like Jesus.

- Have an organized prayer life so that God will strengthen you, focus you, and lead you in every aspect of your work life, especially in your efforts to influence others for Christ.
- Conduct yourself in a manner completely consistent with what God would want...a life beyond reproach. Be strong, yet gentle; action oriented, yet patient; tenacious, yet never bowing to pressure or stress.
- Do your paying job in an excellent way, so that you are respected and looked up to by everyone.
- Love and accept everyone you come in contact with. This is not tolerance, but genuine, active, demonstrated love and acceptance.
- Serve your coworkers, clients, and vendors. Be a

humble, consistent servant whose caring turns the heads of everyone.

- Know what you believe and why you believe it. Have and be constantly pursuing a knowledge of the Scriptures.
- Possess a sensitivity for when to speak and when to just listen.
- Be ready, willing, and able to "give a defense" (see 1 Peter 3:15) of any aspect of your faith when the situation calls for a defense.
- Be a sought-after resource for biblical truth and God's answers to life's tough questions.
- Consistently invest in relationships and build trusted friendships, with the intention and purpose of helping people move one step closer to Christ.
- Be willing to tell your story, in part or in whole, as a witness to what God has done in your life.
- When led by the Spirit, help your trusted friend to step over the line of faith, either by leading him there personally or by bringing him to a pastor or friend who has the tools and experience to lead him into a relationship with Christ.
- Follow through with new believers to help them grow.

Sounds like a tall order, huh? We'll get there, but one step at a time.

Let's look at two overarching facts, facts that are foundational.

1. *Relationships are everything, because people are the only thing that really count in God's eyes.* That's right.

Scripture describes every other thing as temporary—as "wood, hay and stubble" that will disappear. Things we so desperately seek, like good looks, social status, owning cool things, being the boss, beautiful memories and pictures from our travels...all of these disappear through the years of our lives and at our passing. But people go on forever. Which leads to fact number 2...

2. *Everyone will spend eternity somewhere.* We've stopped talking much about sin, hell, and eternal separation from God. So it shouldn't surprise us that our workmates have less of a felt need to be saved from that fate. But Scripture hasn't changed. We read in Revelation 20:15:

"If anyone's name was not found written in the book of life, he was thrown into the lake of fire."

So being about our Father's business is critically important. We have the opportunity and the responsibility to do everything we can to help others avoid this horrible fate.

Take a look at Colossians 1:10 and fill in below....

We pray this in order that you may live a life _____ _____ ____ _____ and may please him in every way: bearing fruit in every _____ _____, growing in the _____ ___ _____.

We start as we "live a life worthy of the Lord." This takes us back to those attributes of a worker that gain the respect of his coworkers. Then we bear fruit "in every good work." This is where we start to see the results of being intentional. And as we see Him produce this fruit in our workplace, we will grow in our knowledge of Him, how He works in our lives and in the lives of others.

So Why Don't We Do It?

Knowing that being a special agent for God is so important, why don't we do it? There's nothing all that new or revolutionary here, so why is it so hard for us to be intentional for Christ every day?

Our struggle comes as no surprise to our Lord. Let's look at what the apostle Paul said about this struggle. Read Romans 7:15 and transcribe it here.

Does that sound like you? It sure sounds like me! I want to exercise but I don't. I hate eating badly, but I do it anyway. Can you relate?

And isn't that the way we are when the "monkey" shows up? We want to be out there for Christ; we really do! But we blow it, we wimp out, or even worse, we preach our coworkers a sermon that drives them away.

There are at least three explanations for why we blow it.

1. **We forget.** We're much less dangerous to Satan when we're busy, and when we're busy, we just forget. "Forget about God, after all He's done for me?" How could we do that? Unfortunately, we do it all the time! And we're not the first generation to be guilty either.

In the Old Testament, we see the pattern repeated over and over. God's people turn away from Him…a crisis situation comes and God bails them out…they fall down and worship God in gratitude and wonder… they forget about God and turn away from Him again…and so on.

2. **We're afraid.** We think we'll offend someone, or we'll hurt our reputation among our colleagues. We don't know what to say. We aren't confident about when we should speak up or keep quiet. We feel woefully inadequate when it comes to knowing Scripture. We may even have a few things we've done or said that we're ashamed of, so we're afraid that people will think our walk doesn't match up with our talk.

3. **We're alone.** We're trying to do good things for God without talking to Him about them. We haven't taken the time to pray for ourselves nor for the people whom we work with. We know that we are supposed to be acting as a special agent for God, but we haven't asked Him what He would have us do nor gotten His instructions as to how we're supposed to do it.

Your "Gratitude Bucket"

What will it take to get us on track consistently in our daily lives at work? What will it take for us to be intentional…to remember and not forget…to not be afraid? What will it take to make organized prayer a daily part of our routine?

The answer is a humble heart that is surrendered to the Lord that realizes that it's all about God.

How does one get a humble heart? Well, there's a high road

and a low road to humility. Let me describe them both, and you'll relate.

The low road is through brokenness. Many if not most Christians come to a humble heart through brokenness. We go our own way in life, regardless of how we were raised or what we were taught as children, and at some point it all falls apart. It's a job crisis, a marital crisis, a health crisis, a family crisis, a financial crisis...it's some set of circumstances that brings us to our knees. We find that we can't make it on our own, and God is there for us. He delivers us, and we are forever changed because of it. God is real and we know it—maybe for the very first time—because He showed up in our life and our circumstances and He got us through. He restored us, and we now depend on Him. Our "gratitude bucket" is full and running over.

If the low road describes your path to the humble heart, stop right here and write a quick thank-you note to God. Remind Him of the crisis you were in, how you got into the situation, how He came through for you in that moment, and how His deliverance has changed your life ever since. Don't make Him any promises; just thank Him for giving you a humble heart through brokenness. Don't forget to sign it!

Dear God,

Thanks again,

The high road to a humble heart is one of gratitude. Some of us have been raised in Christian homes and in the church. We've never strayed all that far from the straight and narrow, so it's hard for us to detail the time when we were "broken." Sometimes, that makes it harder for us to see God's hand in our lives. Here's an exercise for you if you can't specify when you were broken.

There are two columns below; one is titled "Blessings," the other is titled "What If." Take a few minutes and, in the first column, list all of the blessings you have been given—the people, events, experiences, accomplishments, lessons, and even material things that you are most thankful for. You might even do this on another sheet so you won't run out of room.

When you've finished your Blessings list, then think about what might have been. In the What If column, write the opposite of what you wrote in the Blessings column. For example, suppose you're grateful for the blessing of good health. In the What If column, list how it *could have been*. You could have kidney problems, requiring weekly dialysis treatments, for example. We will all probably list salvation among our blessings, but have we ever thought about what the consequences would have been had He not saved us? Visualize them and write them down.

Spend whatever time it takes to think through and list the opposites of what you have been blessed with and list those outcomes in the second column.

Blessings	What If?

Do you see God's hand in your life? Do you see what could have been, were it not for Him? Do you see the blessings and protection He's provided for you? Aren't you grateful for what He's done and what He keeps on doing for you?

Read James 1:17. Where does every gift come from?

Read Matthew 7:11. Think about how much you enjoy giving good gifts to your children. What does that say about God giving us what we need?

Reflecting upon what God has done for us as well as what He's protected us from fills up our gratitude bucket. And when it starts to overflow, we find the energy and focus to pray for others, to love and serve them, and to become intentional for God in every aspect of our lives. We're ready to make our lives a praise to Him and, fueled by our overwhelming gratitude, we'll be motivated to be about our Father's business every day.

New Blessings You'll See

When we take on our second job as special agent for God, we begin to receive new blessings that we've never had nor experienced. These blessings are simply not available to those who stop at phase one and never make the transition to an others-focused Christianity. These blessings are described in Scripture, so let's dig them out so we'll remember them.

1. **You will have peace.** Maybe for the first time in our adult lives, we know that we're doing what Jesus told us to do, we're doing His will, and He is smiling. We can have a peace so deep, it can't really be described or understood.

   Read John 14:27. What kind of peace can we have?

2. **You will be free from guilt.** All of your Christian life, you've felt guilty for not witnessing. When you start to be intentional for Christ and follow the process that we will cover in this study, you'll be free from guilt forever.

   Read Galatians 5:1. For what has Christ set us free?

3. **You will be respected** The members of the body of Christ—the church—are connected in a mysterious and supernatural way. When you commit yourself to the life of a disciple, and your words and actions begin to line up behind that calling, you'll gain respect among other believers and among unbelievers as well. Authenticity brings respect, even when people don't believe what you believe.

   Read Proverbs 3:3–4. What will we have if we never let love and faithfulness leave us?

4. **You will gain rewards in heaven.** Most of us are so busy doing our thing here on earth that we never even focus on heaven. We joke about getting another star in our crown without ever thinking about what

that means. We think, "It's going to be so great just to be in heaven, what would I do with a reward beyond that?"

Read Revelation 4:10–11. What will we do with our rewards in heaven?

So to summarize, we're called to be active followers of Christ as we do our paying jobs. We have been assigned to be special agents for God in our work nation. We will succeed in our endeavors if we pray, then obey. That way, we're following God's lead in the things we do and the relationships that He leads us into. We will forget, we'll be afraid, and we'll blow it over and over, but He is always there, encouraging us and leading us back into the fray. When we obey His call to live phase two of the Christian life—to become focused on others in addition to ourselves—we get blessings that are extraordinary. We'll have peace, we'll be free of guilt, we'll be respected, and we'll have rewards in heaven that we can give back to Him as an offering of gratitude.

Questions for Discussion

1. Think about the people you have observed attempting to be evangelists and disciple makers in your work environment. Describe some of the good, the bad, and the ugly that you've seen.

2. The idea that we have two jobs is probably a new one to you. If disciple making or being a special agent for God were the *only* job you had in your office, what would you do differently?

3. The movement from a faith that is I-focused to one

that is others-focused is a huge step. If you took the total amount of energy that you expend on God in an average day, what percentage of that would be spent on phase-one or I-focused things and what percent would be phase two or others-focused? From a practical point of view, what steps will you take to change those percentages?

4. Which path brought you to the humble, surrendered heart that is ready to be about our Father's business? Was it the low road of brokenness or the high road of gratitude? Explain.

5. As you wrote your thank-you note to God, or as you listed your blessings and the what-ifs that could have been, what went through your head? Jot down the thoughts that came to you as you did this exercise and prepare to share them with the group.

WEEK THREE: RELATIONSHIPS ARE THE "ONE THING"!

Read pages 56–86 in *About My Father's Business*.

Principles and Truths for This Week

1. Actively accepting people is a huge part of having influence for Christ at work.
2. Developing your Intentionality Map will help you focus on people and next steps.
3. Focused, consistent prayer is a necessity if we are to make a difference.
4. Think steps…next steps!

Memory Verse for Week Three

> A new command I give you: Love one another. As I
> have loved you, so you must love one another. By this
> all men will know that you are my disciples, if you
> love one another.
>
> JOHN 13:34–35

Building Your Intentionality Map

Following the instructions on pages 58 through 69 of *About My Father's Business,* create your Intentionality Map, or IMAP. You may want to download the IMAP from our Web site at www.amfb.com. Click the tab labeled Downloads.

The IMAP is intended to be a starting point for becoming intentional for Christ in your work relationships. It's a first-draft snapshot of the people from your work nation whom God has put on your radar screen. Over the coming weeks, we'll look at aspects of each of the five spiritual profiles that make up the IMAP and discuss things we can do to help everyone in our sphere of influence take his or her next step.

Relationships and Your Sphere of Influence

If we believe that God is omniscient (knows everything) and omnipotent (has unlimited power), then it is not an accident that you work where you work. You may only be there for a season, but you can be sure that you are there for a reason! And the people you work with are a big part of that reason. God has some work for you to do in the lives of the people you work with, and He's going to do some work in you while you're at it.

Read John 13:34–35 (our memory verses for the week).

What's the command from our "Boss"?

If our job is to love others the way He loves us, just how *does* He love us?

Who will know that we're His disciples ("special agents")?

Love is such a popular word these days, yet it's a word that few people can accurately define, and even fewer put any effort to it. Outside our closest friends and family, love is a noun rather than a verb.

We want to turn *love* into a verb when it comes to the people on our IMAP, and we're going to start with two simple steps. If we will train and motivate ourselves to do these two things, we will start a revolution in the hearts of these people— a revolution that might just lead to an overthrow of the current regime (selfishness and sin) and the coronation of a new regime: salvation and righteousness!

Acceptance
Modern-day Christians are not known for their acceptance of

people. We're much more identified with judging people. Deserved or not, we're perceived to be down on people who aren't like us. Christians reject abortion, divorce, drinking, drugs, premarital sex, living together before marriage, pornography, and any religion other than ours. But we must learn to accept (and communicate our acceptance of) people who have done or are currently engaged in the behaviors listed above.

Recognize that this is a list of *decisions* people have made, not kinds of people that we reject. We have to discipline ourselves to accept people who have made these decisions (and many others neither we nor Scripture would agree with).

When you listed your coworkers on your IMAP, did you leave people off because you just don't like them? Or you don't respect them because of their involvement in some of the things listed above? Keep those names at the top of your mind. We'll come back to them in just a minute.

First, let's read the story of Zacchaeus in Luke 19:1–10

Which did Jesus communicate first: love or acceptance (verse 5)?

What change in behavior did Jesus require of Zacchaeus before He demonstrated His acceptance and went to his house to visit?

What changes in behavior did Zacchaeus choose to make after Jesus demonstrated His acceptance?

Acceptance is a powerful thing! We all consciously and sub-consciously gravitate *toward* people and environments where we are *accepted*, and we gravitate *away* from environments of *rejection*.

Think for a few minutes about people on your IMAP that you have issues with. This may include the names you passed over before and chose not to put on your IMAP. List them below in column A. Then jot down in column B just one or two words that describe the issue. "Hothead," "Smart aleck," "Critical," "Know-it-all," "Muslim," "Alternative," "Adulterer," "Pothead," "Punk," "Show-off"—these might be some of the descriptive words that come to mind. Now in column C, jot down one or two words that describe how you could respond to that person the next time you encounter them. "Smile," "Eye contact," "Hug," "Ask about her mother," "Accept," or just the word "Pray." How would Jesus respond to this person? Remember that you're on a mission from God, and your job is to communicate acceptance. What do you do?

A Issue Person	B The Issue	C Your New Acceance Response

You see, our natural tendency is to hang out with people who are like us. It's the old "birds of a feather" concept. Problem is, it's not biblical, and it's not what Jesus taught or modeled. He was a friend of sinners, not to mention tax collectors, lepers, and other societal outcasts. He entered into relationships with those people in order to have influence with them and to accomplish His Father's purpose. We must go and do the same.

Prayer

What greater act of love is there than to think of the name of a coworker and to call out that name to the Creator of the universe? When we start to realize that God has put our coworkers into our lives for some purpose, then we know that we have to pray for them if we are to fulfill it. We will fail miserably if we try to do it on our own or make it up as we go.

Through prayer, God will direct the steps of your relationships with people that you are attempting to influence for Him. Praying for them will change your outlook toward them. It may even make it easier for you to love them when they are radically different from you. More important, prayer can change them, their environment, and the way they see you, God, life, their past, and the future. Remember, it's God who is at work here, "to will and to act according to his good purpose" (Philippians 2:13). We're just special agents doing our job, which includes a lot of praying.

Our goal with people who are apathetic toward spiritual things is to spark an interest—to inspire them to begin a search. We can best do that by:

- living out our faith consistently before them. That means loving, serving, and not judging.

- accepting them just as they are and communicating our acceptance.
- praying for them consistently and purposefully. For those in column A of our IMAP, our prayer is that God would light that spark of interest in Him.
- listening and paying attention to them, so that we can learn what they really believe. Everyone believes in something; it's our job to gracefully and patiently find out what that is for the people on our IMAP.

Remember, we treat everyone we meet and everyone in our sphere of influence as if they were apathetic until we learn otherwise.

Questions for Discussion

1. As you prayerfully listed the names of the people in your work nation on your IMAP, what was your biggest struggle?
2. Contrast the word *acceptance* with the word *tolerance*.
3. Many of us have experienced "divine appointments," where we have prayed for someone, gotten some unction to do something, done it, and then seen some incredible result that could only have come from God's involvement. Jot down highlights of one of those stories that you can share with the group.
4. How do we communicate acceptance to the person who is involved in sin and things we don't condone without communicating our acceptance for their behavior?
5. How long should we stay "in the game" with people on our IMAP?

6. How do we decide to add someone, and how do we decide to take someone off?

WEEK FOUR: GOING ON THE JOURNEY WITH THEM

Read pages 87–111 in *About My Father's Business.*

Principles and Truths This Week

1. People who are beginning to search (the second IMAP category) are interested in spiritual things.
2. They are active in their search for truth. They may be seeking, or they may think that they have found the truth, but it's not in Jesus Christ.
3. We face our need for God when there is disruption in our lives.
4. Our goal as special agents for God is to live and relate in such a way that we earn a position of respect and influence in the lives of those seekers, so that when disruption happens, we'll be positioned to point them to Christ.
5. Telling your own story can be a powerful tool in pointing a seeker to Christ.

Memory Verse for Week Four

You will know the truth, and the truth will set you free.

JOHN 8:32

Hope Rises from Movement!

As a kid, my favorite week of the year was vacation. Even more than Christmas, I loved it when my dad would start to load stuff in the car. Mom had made cookies and bought potato chips for the long ride. There was incredible excitement in the air! "We're getting ready to go!"

That's the excitement that comes when someone you've invested in starts to show an interest in spiritual things. Just as with those childhood vacations, we have no idea where we're going, how long it's going to take, nor what roads we're going to travel on the way. But there's excitement when we're going on a trip. And when Dad is driving, we can relax and enjoy the ride because He knows the way.

Same here! When that spark gets ignited in someone, you can be sure that God is involved. Augustine said "There's a God-shaped hole in every man's heart."

God made us that way. He won't force us to love Him. He won't even force us to look for Him, but He's there, hoping that we'll pursue Him of our own free will. Scripture tells us that's part of why God created us and put us in nations all over the world.

> God did this so that men would seek him and perhaps
> reach out for him and find him, though he is not far
> from each one of us (Acts 17:27).

We want to help those who are beginning to search to find truth, but we can't forget a couple of important facts. Read Titus 2:10, and pay particular attention to the last part of the verse.

What character quality are believers encouraged to exhibit?

He wants us to show we can be fully _____. Why?

Remember, statistics show that more than 80 percent of adults who come to Christ do so through the influence of a trusted friend.

How do we build that trust? By telling the truth, by saying what we're going to do and then doing it, and by being "over the top" in our honesty in every detail of our lives.

Becoming trusted friends with people we don't know very well also involves some diplomacy. We have to become safe to them. They have to know they can share their opinions (including their doubts and heretical questions) with us. We have to earn the right to talk about personal things. Importantly, we must then have the patience to wait until there is an interest—a need to know—and that usually comes after some disruption event.

How can we earn the right to be trusted in such a sensitive area as faith? As Jesus said in Matthew 10:16, "I am sending you out like sheep among wolves. Therefore be as shrewd as snakes and as innocent as doves."

The Greek word used here for *shrewd* means ""thoughtful" or "discreet." God is urging us to pray, to contemplate with Him what the best next step for your friend might be. God wants to help you respond as Jesus would. When He sent us into the work nation, He made a huge promise that we can depend on—that He will always be with us.

James gives us more instruction on what we're to do as we go on this journey with our coworker. Read James 1:19–20.

He tells us to be _____ to listen.

Quick implies eagerness. When others are expressing their opinions and beliefs, are we eagerly listening to what they're really saying, or are we tolerating them and waiting until it's our turn, so we can tell them what *we* believe? That's a huge lesson—don't miss it!

We're to be _____ to speak.

Could it be that His advice to be "slow to speak" is so He can have time to guide us, to show us how to be thoughtful and discreet when we respond? When we say things we wish we hadn't said, isn't it usually because we didn't take time to think about what we said or how it might be received?

We're to be _____ to anger, "for man's anger does not bring about the righteous life that God desires."

This last phrase tells us that we're not going to accomplish anything in our own lives nor in the lives of the people we're trying to influence by allowing ourselves to get angry.

Who hasn't had a heated discussion about religion? It's probably the most volatile subject we can talk about. Yet how many times have you seen someone emerge from one of those discussions (arguments!) saying, "Oh yeah, you know...you're right! I've changed my mind today based on what you said!" Never.

"Going on the journey with them" means that we keep our cool and avoid heated discussions and hot-spot topics. We thoughtfully and discreetly point them to truth, and we do it under God's direction (which is usually a lot slower than we'd like!).

As one wise teacher put it, "Do you want to make a point or build a bridge?" Making a point can get you kicked off the journey; building bridges makes you a valuable traveling companion.

Dialogue vs. Discussion

Think about the word *discussion*. When we "dis" something, we "*discard*" it, or we "*dissect*" things in the biology lab. The last part of the word *discussion* comes from the same root as the word *percussion*. So when we discuss something, we're "hitting it back and forth."

Now, contrast that with the word *dialogue*. *Di*- means "multiple" and -*logue* means "truth"…dialogue is when two are seeking truth together.

You can't create an environment that fosters *dialogue* if you know it all! Read the caution given to us in 1 Corinthians 8:1–3.

Knowledge _____ _____, but love _____ _____.

What does verse 2 say about humility?

If we are "known by God," do we have any pressure to know it all? Why or why not?

When we're going on the trail with someone, we're seeking truth together. Sometimes, we'll get to lead—telling our story, suggesting ideas, books to read, CDs to listen to, etc. But sometimes, they'll be leading—taking the "rabbit trail" off into all kinds of theologies, reading and considering things that you know are wrong. That's when we have to listen and pray, love and accept, and wait for the opportunity to guide them back to the path that will lead to truth. Sometimes, you may even have to read or listen to something that you know is not true in order to help your friend to see the problem. Ask God to protect you and give you His insight as you defend your faith against the deception of the Evil One.

Read Colossians 4:5–6

God instructs us to be _____. Sometimes that means holding back on showing that we're right!

What are our conversations to be full of?

If we're wise in our conversations and full of grace, then we'll know how to answer _____.

Meeting People Where They Are

Paul was an incredible evangelist for Jesus Christ. He sets the standard for leaning toward people, no matter where they are coming from. Read 1 Corinthians 9:19–23 below:

> Though I am free and belong to no man, I make myself
> a slave to everyone, to win as many as possible. To the
> Jews I became like a Jew, to win the Jews. To those under
> the law I became like one under the law (though I myself
> am not under the law), so as to win those under the law.
> To those not having the law I became like one not having
> the law (though I am not free from God's law but am
> under Christ's law), so as to win those not having the
> law. To the weak I became weak, to win the weak. I have

become all things to all men so that by all possible
means I might save some. I do all this for the sake of the
gospel, that I may share in its blessings.

So is Paul telling us to become "chameleons"? To be dishonest? disingenuous?

Not at all. He's just saying to go on the journey with them—
meet them where they are, just as Jesus accepted you and met
you right where you were.

The Journey Ends in Only One Place

With all of this wisdom about how to relate to the seeker in our
workplace, never get confused about the final destination, and
that is faith in Jesus Christ alone. Read the words of Jesus in
John 14:6 and then read Acts 4:12.

If we and our coworkers are to find our way to the Father,
then how will we get there?

In whom is salvation exclusively found? _____

Your Story

Earlier in this study, we reflected on four very specific personal
questions.

1. What was your life like before you trusted Christ?
2. What were the circumstances that drove you to need
   Christ in your life?

3. What happened in the twenty-four hours surrounding your committing your life to Christ?

4. What has your life been like since you became a Christian?

(We learned this pattern for telling our story by reading how Paul told his story to King Agrippa in Acts 26:2–22. Read those verses and you'll clearly see Paul answer these four questions as he tells his story.)

Telling your story may be the most powerful and effective thing you can do to inspire a person who is seeking truth to look closely at Jesus Christ. Why? Here are a few good reasons:

1. No one can argue with your story. What happened, happened! It's impossible for someone to disprove your own personal experience.

2. The invisible meets the visible. While God is invisible, you're not. When you tell the story of how the invisible God made visible changes in *you personally* and the seeker has seen substance of that in how you live, that's powerful evidence that the God you're describing is real.

3. No training is required. Everyone who has encountered Jesus Christ has a story. We can *all* tell our story; we simply need the sensitivity to know the right time and the courage to act.

Scripture tells the story of Jesus healing a man who had been blind from birth (John 9:1–25). After being pounded with all kinds of questions about Jesus (questions to which the man didn't know the answers), he shared one irrefutable truth: "One thing I do know. I was blind but now I see!"

We will never know all the answers, but we do know our

own story. Being willing to take the risk and tell it may be the "billboard" your coworker needs to see to make that final turn toward the destination: a relationship with Christ.

If you've never done it before, if you need to refresh your memory, or if you just need to practice, write out your story and ask God to give you an opportunity to tell it to someone this week.

Questions for Discussion

1. What do you think about the idea that disruption is the catalyst that starts our movement toward God?

2. Think of two situations where you saw the absolute truth either violated or upheld. What impact did these situations have on your thinking and belief system?

3. How do you know when to abandon the journey— to "dust off your sandals" and move on? What does moving on look like?

4. We can actively demonstrate love to those in our sphere of influence by sharing our knowledge, our network, and by showing compassion. What makes this a good investment?

5. Think back to the person who was most influential in your coming to Christ. Did he or she accept you? love you? pray for you? Think about that person's role in your disruption event and how God used them to bring you to Himself. What lessons can you learn and apply to your relationships with seekers or people who are in disruption?

WEEK FIVE: TAKING THEM ON A JOURNEY WITH YOU

Read pages 112–123 in *About My Father's Business.*

Principles and Truths for This Week

1. Believing is a starting point, not an end, for the Christian.
2. Mediocrity is disgusting to the Lord. He wants our whole heart.
3. Our faith can be choked by distractions and things we put before our first love.
4. We are to spur one another on, and we can best do that by inviting others to join us as we pursue God ourselves.

Memory Verse for Week Five

And let us consider how we may spur one another on toward love and good deeds.

HEBREWS 10:24

"Oh Sure, I Believe"

Our country is full of Christians, isn't it? All the surveys say it is. Over 60 percent say they're Christians and almost everyone says they believe in God. (Isn't that almost the same thing?)

"I go to church sometimes." "I'm a member at Saint Mark's." "Oh sure, I believe."

In his book *Mere Christianity,* C. S. Lewis compared passive and active Christianity to the Atlantic Ocean and a map of the Atlantic Ocean. Lots of people have seen the ocean. They know it's real; they've experienced it! They've viewed its expanse and its power with awe. But that's as far as they've gone.

They have only walked on the beach.

If we want to *go somewhere* on that ocean, we need a map. A map gives us the benefit of the experience of thousands of people who have traveled the Atlantic before us. "As long as you are content with walks on the beach, your own glimpses are far more fun than looking at a map. But the map is going to be more useful than walks on the beach if you want to get to America," wrote Lewis.

We need both the ocean and the map—belief in Christ and a journey to join Him on! We need the awe of God, particularly of the love that He has for us. But we also need to respond to that love—to go somewhere with it, and for that we need a map (and a few other things too, but we'll come to those in a minute).

The Maze of Mediocrity

Jesus warned us about "beach walking." He knew that our awe of the ocean could fade as we became immersed in life. Read Luke 8:14.

What chokes the faith of believers?

When and where does it happen?

When a plant fails to mature, what are the consequences?

Jesus also knew that we would try to mature, to earn His approval by creating "maps" that would tell people how to be holy. Jesus personally saw and experienced this kind of religiosity as He saw the Pharisees reduce God to an impossible formula of rules and laws. Because we can't sustain an emotional passion for God *and* because we can't measure up to the performance requirements of following the map, we give up on both and fall into mediocrity, with predictable results. Read Matthew 5:13.

Who did Jesus call "the salt of the earth?"

What is salt that has lost its saltiness?

What happens to salt when it loses its saltiness?

Our Christian faith can become useless, "thrown out" (implying that it's put someplace where it's not in the way) and "trampled on by men" (meaning it's not valuable enough to use, protect, or defend). Does that describe the faith of anyone you know?

In Revelation 2:4 and 3:15–16, He graphically describes His reaction to Christians who have "forsaken [their] first love" and become "lukewarm."

How does He know that we're "neither cold nor hot"?

How does mediocrity or being lukewarm about Jesus make God feel?

Why is God's reaction to mediocrity so strong?

Remember, the opposite of love isn't hate; it's apathy! God isn't surprised by our love response to Him, nor is He shocked when people reject Him. That's an exercise of the free will that God gave us. It's the in-betweeners who make Him sick!

What's Our Assignment?
Just as with apathetics and with those who are beginning to search, we're charged with loving and serving these "confessing" Christians. We're often tempted to judge nominal Christians because they don't do the things we do. And as we said earlier, people are attracted to people who accept them, but we avoid those who judge and reject them. Read Romans 14:3.

What are we told *not to do* when fellow believers don't subscribe to the same religious practices that we do?

What has God done for both?

Keeping our mouths shut about nonessential elements of Christian doctrine helps build bridges with fellow believers!

Scripture goes on to give us three very specific instructions or assignments regarding relationships with "confessing" Christians. Read Hebrews 10:23–25. The three assignments are to:

1. "hold _____ to the hope we profess."
   We keep on "living out loud" a life that is attractive to all who know us.
2. "consider how we may _____ _____ _____
   on toward love and good deeds." It's our job to figure

out how to encourage other Christians toward love for God, and toward good deeds for people.

3. "not give up _____ _____." We're challenged to stay in the game with other Christians. We can't encourage other Christians if we aren't connected to them in ongoing relationships.

"Follow Me" Means You

As usual, the answer is found by looking at what Jesus did. He invited His disciples to *follow* Him. Jesus went places and took His disciples with Him almost everywhere He went. As they followed along—often simply observing, sometimes participating, sometimes asking questions—their faith matured. Did they have their setbacks? Sure they did. But all except one spent their lives spreading the gospel after Jesus was no longer physically present, and most died as martyrs as a result.

There are thousands of workplace Bible studies in almost every city. Find one and invite your confessing Christian friend to go with you. If you can't find one, ask him to join you in starting one. There's almost nothing better to inspire a passive Christian to become active than regular Bible study with trusted friends. It is so easy to tell someone about a study, to say "you should go." But it's a hundred times more effective to say "come with me" and bring them.

Invite your Christian friends to get involved with you in your ministry activities. Don't just tell them about the short-term mission trip—sign up to go and invite them to go with you. Invite them into your small group; "as you go," they can follow you there. So much of the anxiety of new and challenging environments is reduced when they can go with their trusted friend.

Bring them to special events at your church, even if you know they come from a different denominational tradition. Explain that you're not "proselytizing"—you just want to share a particular sermon, service, performance, or speaker with them.

Sometimes their faith can be ignited by involvement in a musical or drama production. Volunteer for things that are of genuine interest to you and your friend. Thousands are involved in Habitat for Humanity and similar projects. There are camping ministries, Young Life and Student Venture ministries for high schoolers, and all kinds of opportunities to get involved with college students and internationals. This has to be authentic, not conjured up. So check out things you're already doing or interested in and invite them to join you. Natural…low pressure… but on purpose.

Pray and Obey

Remember, the process is the same: pray for your "confessing Christian" coworkers; develop relationships with them; love and serve them. Ask God for instructions as to how He would have you spur them on, then obey whatever He tells you to do. Don't put pressure on them, and don't put pressure on yourself. Pray and obey. That's it: pray and obey.

When you ask God to show you projects that you can connect your "C" (confessing Christian) friends to, don't be surprised when He does. Connecting them to a "cause" can be catalytic to their faith, launching them into growth mode and moving them from phase one to phase two—from passive to active, from mediocrity to excellence. And along the way, you'll get the blessing of knowing that God used you—especially you—to create another developing disciple.

Questions for Discussion

1. How do you identify the "chosen frozen" in your workplace?
2. What kinds of things choke our faith at work? What can we do to keep it vibrant and growing?
3. We often relate spurring one another on to encouraging someone. How can we "build courage into" someone who has been shy and retreating about their faith in Jesus Christ?
4. What has been your biggest challenge in becoming more active and others-focused in your faith?

WEEK SIX—THE FULLY DEVOTED CHRIST FOLLOWER

Read pages 124–170 in *About My Father's Business*

Principles and Truths for This Week

1. Many people are confused, thinking that Christianity is an "it," that is, something you do or a set of principles.
2. Going public or telling others about your faith is a key first step in becoming a "developing disciple."
3. Learning and applying God's Word is a must-do for growth in our faith.
4. Prayer brings God into current reality for us and allows us to have an interactive relationship with Him.
5. The distinguishing characteristic of excelling Christians is their intentionality for seeing others move one step closer to Christ.

6. We are partners with God in our efforts to work in the lives of people.
7. Connecting with other Christians fuels our growth through encouragement and accountability.

Memory Verse for Week Six

Have I not commanded you? Be strong and courageous. Do not be terrified; do not be discouraged, for the LORD your God will be with you wherever you go.

JOSHUA 1:9

Getting Personal

Having religion is easy. It's something you do, and everyone can learn to do it. Anyone can learn "churchspeak." We can become master church attenders by knowing when to stand up, sit down, kneel, and read the right paragraph out loud.

Many confessing Christians depersonalize faith. "I believe in *it,*" they say. It's just so much harder to refer to "Him." We can talk about church or our set of beliefs as an inanimate "it." But we struggle to refer to "Him" because that's a transition from a thing to a person, and that's the defining difference of Christianity.

In fact, it's really easier in our culture to have a religion than to not have one. The questions are easier to answer. "Oh yes, I'm Catholic" or "I'm Jewish" or "I'm Christian"...all those labels roll off the tongue pretty easily.

But Christianity isn't a label; it's not even something you do. It's something that you *are,* and it's derived from Someone you know. When our faith is mature, it's definitional. Our real-time, interactive relationship with the living God becomes the center of our lives every day. He holds major mind share, and our every thought and action is touched by that interactive relationship. He prompts us to pray, He causes us to wince in our souls when we are insensitive or mean to someone. He brings a tear to our eyes when we see His hand in a situation or a sunset that reminds us of how much He loves us. When we look for Him, we'll see that He's there all the time, making Himself known in all kinds of ways, big and small.

The path to this meaningful, daily, personal relationship with Christ begins when we first truly believe in Him. Look at Romans 10:9.

Our first instruction is to _____ _____ _____ _____ "Jesus is Lord."

But we're also reminded that we must "_____ _____ _____ that God raised him from the dead, [and we] will be saved."

There are no magic words that take us to heaven. Saying the words *and* believing in our hearts will.

And so it is, and so it stays with so many of our fellow Christians. They cheat themselves out of so much by stopping with their salvation and failing to develop in their relationship with their heavenly Father.

Going Public

Step one in becoming a developing disciple is to let people know that you are one. That can be a huge challenge for Christians...especially new believers and especially new adult believers. It's the "what will people think?" syndrome. We can rock along in our "chosen frozen" state and nobody is going to notice us or ask us any questions. But when we start talking openly about Jesus Christ, and the difference He makes in our lives, it will draw attention to us, and we'll have to either go public or run and hide. Jesus anticipated this and gave us a clear picture of the consequences of the decisions we make in those moments of truth. Read Matthew 10:32–33 and answer these questions.

What does Jesus promise to do for those who acknowledge Him before others?

What are the consequences of disowning Him before others?

The first hurdle we have to get over in moving from confessing Christian to developing disciple is to let others know that we are committed to living our lives for Jesus Christ.

So What Is a Developing Disciple?

From Colossians 2:6–7, we see an order for developing as a disciple. Look up those verses and jot down what you think is meant by each word set....

First: "received Jesus Christ"

Second: "continue to live in Him"

Third: "rooted and built up in him"

Fourth: "strengthened in the faith as you were taught"

Fifth: "overflowing with thankfulness"

The roots of our faith are found in the Bible. That's where we learn about God, the ways of God, and the road map for our lives, Jesus Christ. So we can't become developing disciples without getting rooted in God's Word.

Anyone can pick up a Bible, read it, and grow. Millions do it every day. But there is so much more to be gained by studying the Bible with a group, sharing insights and experiences, and allowing the Spirit to teach. In addition, there are thousands of books that record the insights of brilliant people who have spent their whole lives translating, studying, and interpreting the Scriptures. We have such leverage to get the benefit of lifetimes of learning, all within our grasp—if we will only commit the time to read.

But Bible knowledge, in and of itself, doesn't make one a developing disciple. Jesus pointed this out to the religious leaders of His day in John 5:37–40. Read those verses now and answer the questions below.

What's the difference between studying the Scriptures and having the Word "dwell in you?"

We can't "have life" by simply studying the Scriptures; we must _____ _____ _____ to have life.

Developing disciples distill the principles taught in Scripture and apply them to their everyday lives. But they're only able to effectively do that as they pray and ask God to teach them.

To Pray or Not to Pray

To grow up "in Him" says that we grow up in His image. We can read the words of Jesus in the Bible. We can even get a mental picture of how Jesus responded in different situations that might look like the ones we face. But if we are going to "have life, and have it to the full" (John 10:10), we are going to have to come to Him, early and often. The developing disciple is in constant dialogue with God, praying for Himself and for others, praying for understanding, for patience, for wisdom, even praying that God will give him enough faith to believe that his prayers are going somewhere.

Read Ephesians 6:18 and respond to these questions:

Does He really mean to pray "on all occasions?" Why or why not?

What are some of the kinds of prayers we can make?

To "always keep on praying" means nonstop. Is that reasonable?

Why do you think we are reminded to "be alert"?

To become learners and followers of Christ, we must always be alert for the application of Scripture to the situation that we're in or the decision that we're facing. God is alive and interactive. He's responsive to our prayers. He wants us to learn. And most of all, He wants us to emulate His beloved Son in every aspect of our lives. So God, through the Holy Spirit, is actively involved in our development. He prompts, He challenges, He teaches, He flashes questions into our heads. Jesus explained this as part of the job of the Counselor in John 14:26. Read that verse and answer below.

In whose name will the Counselor be sent?

What will the Counselor teach us?

What will the Counselor remind us of?

It's easier for God to remind us of things Jesus said when we've heard them at least once before. We can only hear them the first time by reading and remembering Scripture.

Isn't it cool that God promises to be involved in our development, and all He asks is that we be involved first?

Fellowship—the Source of Accountability and Encouragement

We all do better when someone is watching. Fellowship brings accountability, and when developing disciples meet together there is a natural accountability that occurs. Notice what has happened through the first five weeks of this study: people have shown up; they've studied their Bibles; they've discussed different ideas and strategies for becoming more like Jesus. Would that have happened to the same degree if you had taken this study on "all by your lonesome?" Not likely. Take a look at Ephesians 4:15–16 and answer below.

What is the "whole body?"

What is God's role in the development of the body and the disciples who make up the body?

Describe how the word *synergy* applies to these verses.

Along with accountability, being connected (or "in fellowship") with other disciples gives us a source of encouragement. We're affirmed when we see others trying to do the same thing we're trying to do. Hearing of their successes *and* their setbacks can give us the courage to keep on keeping on! Read 1 Thessalonians. 5:11:

"Therefore encourage one another and build each other up, just as in fact you are doing."

Look at the "Ds" on your IMAP and ask God to show you the name of the person He would have you encourage today with a call or an e-mail. Do it now, and write the name of the person here _____.

Developing Disciples and Outsiders

When we make the decision to follow Christ, I mean really follow Christ, we embark on a new life of adventure. All the things we've been talking about are pretty out there: reading and memorizing Scripture, praying all the time (and about everything), meeting with other Christians to challenge and encourage them. But nothing is as scary as beginning to think about sharing our faith with outsiders. It's a harrowing thought for many of us— the prospect that we might actually tell our own personal story or, scarier still, lead someone to Christ.

All of these things take courage and faith—sometimes what seems like blind faith. But read what God promises in Isaiah 42:16:

> I will lead the blind by ways they have not known,
>   along unfamiliar paths I will guide them;
> I will turn the darkness into light before them
>   and make the rough places smooth.
> These are the things I will do;
>   I will not forsake them.

Isn't it comforting to know that while we're struggling to know what to do, how to share, when to speak up, and when to stay silent, the God of the universe is quietly leading the outsiders in our lives down a path that leads to Him. Sure, they can remain in the opt-out mode and reject Him, but that's not our responsibility. We're to become mature disciples ourselves as we love and accept them. Then we're to pray and obey what He urges us to do. We rest, knowing that God is at work, drawing our colleagues toward Himself, and that it is His will for all to come to know Him.

Gut Check

In many cases, the highest hurdle we have to clear in our walk with Christ is sharing our faith with others. As we said earlier, we've mistakenly defined evangelism or sharing our faith as an event, when it's really a process. Since God is responsible for the outcome, the question is really whether we will have the courage to try, to focus on others, and become *intentional* in our prayers and relationships. Virtually everything we do in a relationship can have a spiritual motive, and when it does, we are on task to glorify God in our lives. When we *intentionally* love, *intentionally* serve, *intentionally* accept, *intentionally* forgive, *intentionally* invite, *intentionally* pray for a person at work with the motive (or intention) of obeying and pleasing God, then we are about our Father's business in that activity. It's that broad, and that simple! Becoming an excelling "E" means that you've accepted the job of pursuing the hearts of men and women for Christ, not just enjoying the benefits of Christianity yourself.

Joining Forces

When we take the first step and tell God that we're going to start intentionally building relationships for His purposes, He often gives us help. That help usually comes through another excelling Christian who cares for others as you do.

There is nothing quite like having a friendship with another excelling Christian where working together to make a difference for Christ is central to the relationship. Read 1 Corinthians 3:5–9, where Paul described his partnership with Apollos.

What bound Paul and Apollos together (verse 8)?

How would each be rewarded?

With whom are we "fellow workers"?

So our partnership isn't just with other excelling Christians, it's also with God Himself. Isn't it awesome to know that we are working in partnership *with* God, not just trying to do something good *for* God! We are united with Christ on our mission from God.

Read Philippians 2:1–2.

God wants us to be _____ minded.

God wants us to have the _____ love.

God wants us to be one in spirit and _____.

Every challenge in life is easier to face when we have partners. Yes, Jesus is always with us, but it gives us courage to step out when we know other people are going with us. Read Ecclesiastes 4:9–12 and fill in your answers below.

What are four reasons that it's better to have "partners" in your workplace ministry?

1.

2.

3.

4.

Because we are working in partnership with God, we can trust that He will meet all of our needs. Sometimes we find ourselves in a job or an organization where it feels like we're the only Christian in the place. But we must be patient and alert. God rarely sends us out alone, and in time, we'll likely find other Christians who are as anxious to find us as we are to find them. Read Mark 6:7 and answer below.

How did he send His disciples out?

How did He equip them for the mission?

God recognizes the strength that comes from partnership. He will never abandon us nor leave our needs unmet. If you're alone in your organization and feel like the Lone Ranger, pray fervently. Ask God to lead you to one of His other faithful followers nearby. Keep on asking, and be alert for His answer. He or she may not be who you expect!

Another huge reason to have partners is for prayer. When you are going to lunch with someone and you're planning to challenge them toward the next step in his or her faith, how awesome it is to be able to quickly ask for and get focused prayer from someone who wants your colleague to take that next step as much as you do. We're encouraged to team up in praying, and we're reminded of God's promises in Matthew 18:19–20. Read them now, and respond to the questions below.

What does God promise about your prayers when "two or three" gather to ask?

Who will be there with you when come together in His name?

The Greatest Job Ever!
In survey after survey, employees tell us they care about three things.

1. They want to do work that matters—work that has purpose and meaning.
2. They want to belong—to feel that they are a part of something special and that someone cares about them.
3. They want to make a contribution—to make a difference and not just be "a part of the machinery."

In these weeks, we have reviewed a process that can give these three things—and a lot more!—to everyone who works. What we do matters for all of eternity—for us and for the people in our sphere of influence. We belong to a great kingdom that is invisible today but will someday be visible and tangible. We're valuable members of God's team of disciples, whom He wants to become disciple makers.. We're His special agents to our work nation. He cares about us so much that He goes with us every day, in everything we do. And we have the opportunity to make a huge contribution, one that we have been uniquely selected for and positioned to make. We have the opportunity to live a great adventure in God-led relationships, and make a difference for Him with people who may never be touched by a church or a vocational minister.

What is our "coefficient of regret," the likelihood that we will end up with regrets if we choose *not* to try?

Pretty high.

And what is our probability of success if we sign on to be about our Father's business?

One hundred percent.

We can fail only if we don't try.

God will use whatever you give Him. Give Him a lot. No, give Him everything!

Questions for Discussion

1. Name some of the visible, public activities that developing disciples will be found being involved in.

2. Describe a lie that the Enemy has used to keep you from growing in your faith. What was the fear that his lie paralyzed you with? What have you done (or what must you do) to break free from that fear and get on with being about our Father's business?

3. Now that you've read *About My Father's Business* and completed this study, what holds you back from being "full on" for Him with the people you work with?

INTENTIONALITY MAP

Apathetic	Beginning To Search	Confessing Christian	Developing Disciple	Excelling Christian
Daryl	Bob P.	Doug	Juliet	Andy
Steve	Chuck	Jeff	Paul	Steve
Robert	Craig	Randall	Bob D.	John
Julia	Sam	Dave	Fred	Charlie
	Al	Ken	Tim	Bill
	Steve	Craig		

A leader's guide for this study, including discussion helps and answers to the fill-in questions, is available at www.amfb.com at no charge.

NOTES

1. "Major Religions of the World Ranked by Number of Adherents," *Adherents.com*, 6 September 2002. http://www.adherents.com/Religions_By_Adherents.html (accessed 1 October 2004).

2. William Carr Peel and Walt Larimore, *Going Public with Your Faith* (Grand Rapids: Zondervan, 2003), 89–92.

3. Ed Silvoso, *Prayer Evangelism* (Ventura, CA: Regal Books, 2000), 42.

4. See www.barna.org/FlexPage.aspx?Page=Topics.

5. Os Hillman, "The Faith at Work Movement: Opening 'The 9 to 5 Window,'" *Christianity Today.com*. http://www.christianitytoday.com/workplace/articles/issue9-faithatwork.html (accessed 8 October 2004).

6. John Eldredge, *The Journey of Desire* (Nashville: Thomas Nelson Publishers, 2000), 7.

ABOUT THE AUTHOR

After twelve years as a telecommunications executive, James R. (Regi) Campbell started his own sales and marketing consulting firm. He was soon recruited to be the CEO of a start-up company that grew to more than two hundred employees and was acquired by a large telecommunications firm. Altogether, Campbell has been involved in starting and/or running four very successful companies, one of which employed more than thirteen hundred people. He is a former "High Technology Entrepreneur of the Year" in Georgia.

Regi Campbell is a graduate of the University of South Carolina and holds an MBA from its Moore School of Business. He is a key investor and manager of Tax Partners, LLC, a successful business process outsourcing company. He also serves on the board of High Tech Ministries, an organization that creates workplace Bible studies in Atlanta's high tech community and sponsors a High Tech Prayer Breakfast that draws almost two thousand participants.

Campbell knows about being a marketplace minister. Through his involvement with Andy Stanley and the team at North Point Community Church, one of America's largest and fastest growing churches, Campbell has found a pattern to organize and communicate his insights in ways that are easy to understand and apply. The result is About My Father's Business.

"Many people in the marketplace live with guilt or fear about sharing their life in Christ with others. Regi Campbell opens the door to clarity and understanding on how to live out our faith among our cola-borers in the marketplace. I highly recommend this book. I am confident it will be life changing."

ALAN ANDREWS,
PRESIDENT, US NAVIGATORS

"Regi Campbell has been offering analysis and guidance on this topic for years, and with this book he has helped all who desire a more inte-grated life of faith and work."

DR. STEPHEN R. GRAVES,
FOUNDER OF LIFE@WORK AND CORNERSTONE CONSULTING GROUP

"Tensions and challenges are real for Christians who want their work to be a ministry, and readers will find real answers that enable them to be about their Father's business every day of the week."

SARA MOULTON REGER,
IBM RESEARCH

"When I get advice on how to live a life with impact, I want to hear it from someone with a track record. And Regi Campbell has one. A suc-cessful business leader and a committed follower of Christ, he has discovered a practical and powerful way to fuse a walk of faith with a life at work. You don't have to leave your faith in the parking lot when you arrive at work Monday through Friday."

BOB RECCORD,
PRESIDENT, NORTH AMERICAN MISSION BOARD, SBC

"My word of caution is simple: this book may revolutionize the way you see your work. If you take Regi's words seriously, you'll see your job as a mission, not merely a marketplace. I pray that you not only read, but also practice these principles."

TIM ELMORE,
PRESIDENT, GROWING LEADERS, INC.;
VICE PRESIDENT, EQUIP

BETWEEN ENEMIES

By Amos Elon:

Journey through a Haunted Land
The Israelis: Founders and Sons